SKIING WITH PENGUINS

A FAMILY'S CHASE TO BREAK A WORLD RECORD

BY

JORDAN LIPP

ISBN: 978-0-9774619-1-2 (paperback)
ISBN: 978-0-9774619-2-9 (epub)

Cover Design by Zoe Kaatz
www.zoekaatz.com

Table of Contents

Dedication

This book is dedicated to all the strangers who had to sit next to my kids and me on ski lifts over the past many years. I appreciate you happily tolerating my kids singing the Pina Colada song, telling everyone on the lift about the dreams they had the night before, and endlessly debating between them if Silverton or Taos is their favorite ski area. Thank you for putting up with us.

Acknowledgments

To do a proper acknowledgement would take up a book in and of itself. No adventure of this scope can be accomplished without countless people. I'll try to keep the acknowledgments short, with my endless apologies to those left out.

Let me start with the acknowledgements with the people overseas who assisted in our record chase. The White Desert team (especially Patrick Woodhead, Mindy Roberts, Sam Beaugey, Catherine Stott, and Kayleigh Woodman) made our Antarctica ski in February 2022 possible, and I cannot thank them enough. Gary and Violet Barrett's generosity and kindness in unexpectedly welcoming us to their home and giving us a place to live during our extended stay in Cape Town was wonderful. Likewise, Kanyisa Tembani's assistance and emotional support during our issues in Cape Town were incredibly appreciated. Geoff Brookes provided advice on the Australian ski areas and welcomed us in Sydney. Sadly, I've lost the names of the strangers who graciously helped us when our car broke down in Cooma, Australia, to whom we are so grateful for their assistance. Rees Automotive Repairs in Cooma slotted us in after hours to fix our car allowing us to return to the United States the next day as planned and kept me in good favor with my wife, as opposed to being stuck in Australia. Hector Silva provided excellent advice on skiing in the Andes. Camila Rodriguez and Christian Bauza graciously welcomed us to Valle Nevado – and in spite of the myriad of work getting the ski area prepared for opening day – provided us with time to make turns at Valle Nevado. And Jorge Kozulj, our ski mountaineering guide in Patagonia and the Antarctic Peninsula approached ski guiding children with enthusiasm, hard efforts, and a nearly fatherly attention to Keira and Maddock. We could not have asked for a better ski mountaineering guide.

Domestically, the list of people to thank is just as long (and my apologies to the Canadians listed below for lumping you together with Americans in this domestic category). Our December 2022 ski of Antarctica could not have occurred without the active and enthusiastic support of Doug Stoup and his team at Ice Axe Expeditions. Jake Morrison and his team at Quark Expeditions were wonderfully welcoming and helpful in supporting two children on an otherwise all adult expedition. Professor Brian Rosser provided excellent advice, as he always does, in getting the kids ready to ski in Africa, as well as assisting with paperwork. Kevin Ong provided the key recommendations to give us the bravery to start travelling with young children in the first place (when you read about the *travel fairy* later in the book, you'll understand this reference). Cindi Boettcher White kindly welcomed our accomplishment with open arms, and the White family's prior amazing world record made our chase possible. Paperwork for these sorts of travels and record chases seem endless, and we were helped at various points by Jennifer Smith, Matt Hofmeister, and my niece Zoe Kaatz. As our record chase gained public attention, the various local and national media outlets who covered the story were all wonderful, and we were particularly appreciative of the team at KDVR in Denver (Fox31 & Channel 2) who took time out of their schedules after the interviews to give Keira (twice) and Maddock (once) behind the scenes tours of their newsroom, control room, and television studios. Considering not a single bag was ever lost, and no flight was cancelled or severely delayed, I should thank United Airlines as well. Keira and Maddock's teachers' patience and assistance with keeping the kids up to date in spite of missed school was critical – thank you to Daphne Anderson, Moss Benke, Michelle Hamilton, Julia McCluer, and Missy Patten.

For the kids to ski all seven continents, they needed lots of training and practice. My three primary backcountry ski buddies (two are fellow ski patrollers and the third is on search & rescue) were amazingly willing to have my kids tag along for multiple backcountry ski trips despite my kids' casual (a/k/a slow) pace on the ascents. One of my ski buddies also arranged kids rock climbing days, and another one joined us for multiple glacier travel and crevasse rescue practice sessions. These three great friends are Ken Dykes, Ben Hogan, and Richard Jones – and preparing the kids for the rigors of skiing on all the continents would have been very difficult without their generous time and patience.

My parents, Dan and Ronnie Lipp, were the first people we told about our plans to chase the world record. They joined us for the non-skiing portions of two of the trips – Australia and South Korea. Keira and Maddock loved having Grandma and Grandpa along for the record chase, and their help was greatly appreciated.

Finally, our family of four were a team who jointly worked to make these adventures happen. While I was the one who put pen to paper to write this account, the account happened because of equal efforts of all four of us. The family team, of whom you're about to read, are my wife Heather, my daughter Keira, and my son Maddock. Heather supported us through every portion of our adventures and joined the kids and me for all the trips except for Keira and my first trip down to Antarctica. Keira and Maddock were as tireless and enthusiastic as Heather and I were. Adults complain about 15-hour long flights. Keira and Maddock did not. They approached training for the rigors and dangers of Antarctica with enthusiasm, excitement, and commitment. The four of us enjoyed the successes together and shared the frustrations of the failures together, as we worked to achieve this feat. I cannot thank Heather, Keira, and Maddock enough.

Introduction

I cannot rest from travel; I will drink life to the lees.
Alfred Lord Tennyson

As we opened the doors to the car in the parking lot of the Oukaimeden Ski Area in Morocco, numerous people converged on our car, each trying to sell us anything and everything. There was a man with a donkey. Another man was pushing us to buy his green tea. A woman kept showing us a basket of local fruit. And a man without ski boots kept demanding that we hire him as a "guide" to show us around the ski area.

While my wife and I were overwhelmed with the situation, our seven-year-old daughter and five-year-old son were both nonplussed. They patiently waited for me to help them put on their ski boots as I tried to ignore the pushy man with the donkey. After all we were in Morocco to ski, not to be the proud new owners (or at least borrowers) of a donkey.

While I've always enjoyed travel, I was not prepared for the adventure of taking my two children – Keira and Maddock – to the ends of the earth to chase a world record. Chasing a record is not easy – there's a reason why a world record is a world record, even if it's an obscure one. And having two children, our goal was not to only break the world record once, but to break it twice – once for each child.

When my wife and I first decided we'd try to take the kids to ski on snow on all seven continents, I would have never guessed the craziness of the ski area parking lot in the Atlas Mountains of Africa. I would never have guessed that we would ski on the inside of a caldera of an active volcano in the South Shetland Islands. I was not prepared for avoiding kangaroos, who have a self-destructive habit in twilight of hopping across the roads, while we were driving to the Snowy Mountains of Australia. I did not expect that my young daughter and I would get quarantined in Africa while trying to get to Antarctica. I did not expect that we would voluntarily be jumping into water technically colder than the freezing point.

To chase the record, we went to places few Americans have seen, and basically no American children have ever seen. We had many adventures – perhaps too many adventures. But what an extraordinary odyssey for a family of four to experience.

The physical beauty of some of the regions in the world we visited are almost indescribable. The sunlight, shadows, mountains, and ice my daughter and I saw while skiing above an ice sheet in Antarctica under the midnight sun was otherworldly. Almost as spectacular, but seen by many more people than the interior of Antarctica, were the towering rocky slopes of the Matterhorn as we skied beneath them. On the other hand, the views in other places, like South Korea and Australia, were more pedestrian, though still pretty. Just as the views differed, the quality of skiing differed from continent to continent. On some continents it was extraordinary. On others, it was rather lousy.

But the point of the travel wasn't just about the skiing and the scenery. We had almost as much fun eating the local cuisines (and for my wife and I, drinking the local wines). I spoke to every local that I could, politely drilling them for information on their lives, their skiing experiences, their views on other countries, and their thoughts on their own country. It was, without doubt, a cultural tour of the world. And a shared passion for skiing allowed locals to open up to me in ways that would not have been possible otherwise.

I was perhaps most fascinated by the cultural microcosm of the varying ski cultures. While I was already intimately familiar with the American and Canadian ski cultures (and generally familiar with the European ski culture) before our travels, our journey took us to places so different than the skiing universe that I knew. In South Korea, the lift operators at the top of the chairlift stood outside the lift shack and bowed to each group of skiers as they unloaded the lifts. At the largest ski area on the continent of Africa, my wife and one French tourist were the only two adult women not wearing either a burka or hijab. And no one, other than our family, was wearing a ski helmet.

While this is just the book of one family's globetrotting adventures, it is more than just a description of skiing – such as the mountains, snow conditions, and ski lifts. It is my description as an outsider of the people, the culture, the cuisine, the alcohol, and the feel of the six continents I do not call home.

I hope this book resonates with non-skiers just as much as it does with skiers. Skiing was only the vehicle for the world record chase. Much of our time on this chase was not spent skiing – but travelling and seeing the world. The starting point for our adventures necessarily began in larger cities. After all, one is all but required to start on each continent at a major metropolitan airport, and thus a big city, before going by plane, car, or boat to the less populated ski destinations. For this record chase we spent time in numerous major world cities – Buenos Aires, Cape Town, London, Marrakesh, Santiago, Seoul, and Sydney – as well as many less populated locations.

In this book, I want to capture not only how I saw the countries and cultures, but how my children perceived them. We went to the same places, but the kids and I saw those places through different eyes and different perspectives.

And in writing this account, I could not help but write about parenting. Teaching children to ski and to travel at the level to break a world record is, unsurprisingly, no easy feat. Teaching them how to emotionally deal with the successes and failures of trying to break a world record and to do something no one has done before is in many ways even more difficult. While our parenting definitively succeeded on the travelling and skiing front, I can only hope we succeeded on the emotional front.

Similarly, this book necessarily must be a rumination on the advantages and pitfalls of setting aggressive goals. And what could be a more aggressive goal in a world populated with eight billion souls than to try to break a world record? To do something the other eight billion and the billions before them have not – regardless of how esoteric that record might be?

While world travel in the current era is relatively safe, skiing in Antarctica is not. The risks are not just hypothermia, frostbite, and the ocean travel. Rather, being in the glaciated environment at the southern reaches of the world, the looming risks are icefall, crevasses, and avalanches. Understanding and managing risks in this inhospitable environment for an experienced adult is one thing. It is an entirely larger challenge when bringing young children into this environment. Training children to have the skiing and climbing skills to thrive in this forbidding continent, teaching them the basics of avalanche and crevasse rescue, and being able to make risk management judgment calls involving children necessarily formed the backbone of our adventures in Antarctica. Discussing training and risk management is thus a focus of several portions of this book.

Trying to have two family members become the youngest person ever to ski on all seven continents is a multi-faceted endeavor. As such, for better or worse, this book necessarily must be as multifaceted as our adventures were – not a simple one-dimensional story, but rather a tale of skiing, travel, culture, mountains, parenting, risk taking, goal setting, public attention, success, and failure – to name only a few of the topics.

I have divided this book into five roughly equal length parts. The first part provides a quick introduction to the four of us, Keira and Maddock's skiing on our home continent of North America, and the genesis of the idea to chase the world record. And this first part will have a few detours along the way on surviving (and enjoying) travel and skiing with young children. The second part will tell the stories of the next four continents we checked off in the order we skied on them – Europe, Australia, Asia, and Africa. Africa will get the most attention as, unsurprisingly, it is the second most unusual and challenging continent on which to ski. Part three of the book tells the story of every aspect of our first round in Antarctica – starting with a primer on the greatest continent on earth, recounting the roadblocks and disappointments, and finishing under the literal Antarctic midnight sun. Part four of the book deals with the media attention our chase began to garner, along with skiing South America, and our reflections on the meaning of a world record chase. The fifth and final part of the book recounts our second time skiing the greatest continent on Earth – skiing next to penguins and icebergs. And of course, after a conclusion, I had to tuck away a few geeky appendices to satisfy my internal ski geekiness. I assume few will have the patience to read all four of these appendices, in spite of how much I may geek out on them.

While the parts of the book, and the chapters within them, more or less follow the timeline of events, I have tried to draft each chapter as a discreet story. I did this as I do not want the reader to feel encumbered by having to finish (or even read) any particular chapter before diving into the next one.

So, here is the story. From enjoying plush ski resorts in the Alps and Rockies, to climbing a nunatak jutting above an ice sheet in Antarctica, this is the retelling of my family's adventures and observations on our journey to attempt to twice break the world record of the youngest person to ski on every continent.

PART 1

THE FIRST CONTINENT AND AN IDEA

Chapter 1

The Cast of Characters (1970s to present)

If life is a dream, let's dream a great dream.

Yuichiro Miura

L et me start this account with an introduction to the four of us, beginning with the two of us who were actually chasing the record.

Keira and Maddock – The heroes of this story were both born in Colorado. Keira was born in May 2012, and her younger brother, Maddock, was born in November 2014. They grew up in Golden, Colorado – a town probably best known as the home of Coors Brewery, nestled at the base of the Rocky Mountains. Golden is either the furthest westerly suburb of Denver, or the first true town of its own to the west beyond Denver's suburbs. It is the perfect location for mountain-lovers with office jobs. In one direction, it's a 25-minute commute without traffic to downtown Denver. In the other direction, without traffic (or snow covered) roads, it's a 45-minute drive to legendary backcountry skiing spots of Berthoud Pass, Jones Pass, and Loveland Pass. In less than an hour and a half, one can access such famous ski areas as Breckenridge, Copper Mountain, Vail, and Winter Park, to name only a few. And this says nothing of the numerous hiking, rock climbing, and biking spots within a fifteen-minute drive of Golden.

Golden is not just convenient, but it is also beautiful and wild. Growing up in a house on the side of Lookout Mountain in Golden, one of Keira's first two-word combinations when she was learning to speak was "elk poop." That was appropriate as there are tons of elk that hang out in our mountainous neighborhood. And they leave their droppings everywhere. More annoyingly, during the fall rut – i.e., the elk's mating season – the male elk's bugling would, not infrequently, wake us up in the middle of the night.

As many people complain about their neighbors, I certainly do not want to join and complain about our four-legged neighbors in Golden. Setting aside their feces, their penchant to wake us up during mating season, and the fact that no one in our neighborhood would be foolhardy enough to grow vegetables in a garden without a fully enclosed fence, the elk were beautiful creatures and noble neighbors.

Fortunately, the typical animals in our neighborhood were mostly limited to people, pets, rabbits, deer, and elk. The more pernicious animals on Lookout Mountain – i.e., bears, mountain lions, and rattle snakes – were rarely seen. We discussed proper protocols with both children in the unlikely event they ran across a bear, mountain lion, or rattle snake. And I was immensely proud of Keira while hiking twenty steps ahead of Maddock and me at age seven, when she heard the rattler for the first time, and reacted perfectly. She promptly hustled out of striking distance of the rattler, and then yelled to Maddock and me: "rattlesnake!"

Not surprisingly, she wasn't nearly as calm and collected when she was three years old, and I pointed out a bear while camping. Somehow, Keira was able to literally climb up my side in under a second. Having been ascended so quickly, I understood what a ladder feels like. Keira was then happy to view the black bear to our left while being perched on my right shoulder. That bear, which she subsequently named "Cindy-Rudolph," became a legend in our four-person family lore.

Keira has always had an adventurous spirit in the outdoors – though much to my chagrin that adventurous spirit never applied to food. Keira's taste in food was simple. If it had melted cheese on it (think pizza, cheeseburger, quesadilla, mac-n-cheese, etc.) she liked it. If it did not, then she didn't like it.

Keira, though sweet, had a particular knack for humorously getting under my skin. Looking in the mirror I once remarked how it seemed like the little hair I had left on my head was quickly turning grey. Keira looked at me and said: "No daddy, your hair isn't grey." With a smile I told her that this was very sweet of her to say, even though my hair was in fact turning grey. She then said: "daddy, your hair isn't grey. Your hair is white." Although I insisted to her my hair was just turning grey, she was adamant that it was turning white – "look in the mirror Daddy, that color is white! Not grey. White!"

For another example, Keira once asked me – "Daddy, in our family, you're the strongest one, right? Then mommy, then me, and then Maddock, right?" After thinking about it for a second, I told her that her order was fair. "Then," she asked, "why does Maddock have the best six-pack stomach, I have the second best one, and you have the biggest belly in the family?"

There's nothing like having such a supportive daughter. But like me, Keira was tough and had grit. In fact, her grit often outshone my own. And we bonded over a passion for skiing (as well as a love of music that drove my wife crazy, such as listening to The Who).

Maddock, two and a half years younger than Keira, was more rambunctious than Keira. He was also the stereotypical boy – turning every toy or object imaginable into a gun or light saber. But he was also super sweet. And as time went on, he became even more adventurous than Keira.

I taught Maddock the protocols in responding to a scary wild animal – i.e., never run, hands in the air to make yourself look bigger, deep voice responding to the animal, and slowly backing away while facing the animal. Right after one of these practices when Maddock was four, we went to visit a neighbor with a large dog. The dog came running up to us, and Maddock, ignoring every bit of our training, turned and fled as fast as his little legs would take him. The dog happily chased Maddock around in circles in the house as Heather and I laughed hysterically (though with a bit of disappointment) at how he seemed to have learned nothing.

But, as he grew, he steadily became more brave and more confident. Considering our world record chase started when he was four and ended when he was eight – the growth during this time was extraordinary. At age four, he was running away from big dogs. By age six, however, if there was a spider or large bug in the house, while Heather shirked away, Maddock wanted to be the one to kill it. By age eight, while in Antarctica, Maddock wanted to be the first one of the four of us to do the polar plunge – to jump into the literally freezing cold ocean. If it was something adventurous, and we would allow it, he always wanted to go first.

Not only was he adventurous in activities, but he was also far more adventurous than Keira with cuisine. He would eat sushi – something Keira would never do as there is no melted cheese on sushi. The food challenges of travelling were never an issue with Maddock.

Keira and Maddock were (and are) good kids. They were sweet natured, usually polite, and good listeners. This was essential to every part of our adventures – whether their cooperation with travel or listening to instructions on the mountain.

Heather and I used to joke that we'd go to the preschool meetings with teachers, and they'd rave about how well behaved our kids were, much to our puzzlement. Mystified, we'd ask them if they were mixing up our kids with their classmates. Were there two different kids named Maddock in the class, one well-behaved and the other one our son – and they were confused between them? But as Keira and Maddock got older, we came to realize and appreciate just how well-behaved both kids were, and what a positive attitude they had towards life. Good reports from teachers no longer shocked us.

These attitudes made them great travelling companions, and quick learners of the myriad of skills needed to ski throughout the world. Of course, kids can't do their adventures alone, so let's turn to the adults.

Heather and me – Heather, my wife, was raised in a very different world than our kids in Golden. But she came from an equally amazing location. Although technically born in California, she moved with her mother and older sister to Hawaii while still a baby. Between the ages of one and twenty, she lived on four different Hawaiian Islands – Maui, Lanai, the Big Island, and Oahu. Unlike many Hawaiian residents, she was anxious to leave these tropical islands, and she moved from Hawaii to Colorado shortly after graduating from college. She began working at a counter of a car rental shop in Colorado, and then slowly started to work her way up in the world of business.

During a series of finance jobs, one employer helped put her through two master's degrees – an MBA and a master's in accounting. Soon she ended up spending several years doing investor relations – the job of explaining to Wall Street why the large public company you work for is worth their investment. It is a natural job for young, good looking, and mathematically inclined businesspeople. Heather perfectly met each of those requirements. This was Heather's job when both Keira and Maddock were born. Heather switched out of investor relations after Maddock was born to focus on finance and management. She continued her rapid ascent in the business world as Keira and Maddock grew.

Beyond a sharp mind and great looks, Heather has a quick wit, of which I am continually jealous. Far more of the zingers in our house come from her than from me. And it was only natural for her to combine her love of wine and sense of humor when she created a wine blog in 2015 – www.10kbottles.com. The wine blog was a fun look at wine and wine tasting. And for every high-end wine tasting that would go into the blog, she'd be sure to balance it out with a funnier wine tasting – such as doing a blind wine comparison of Costco versus Trader Joe's wines.

We jointly wrote a wine book in 2018 on the seemingly dense topic of wine laws. When people would ask about how we jointly wrote the wine book – *Is There Apple Juice in My Wine* – our response was always the same. I wrote the entire first draft of the book in my not-so-exciting prose, and Heather then reworked it to make it funny and readable. I am sure that you, the reader, will regret that Heather did not cowrite this book with me.

If Keira and Maddock got their looks and sense of humor from their mother, they got their love of the mountains from me. I grew up in a far less interesting location than either Heather or our kids. I grew up in the hills of western New York. My father, who ski patrolled on the weekends at the local ski area, started me skiing when I was two. When I was sixteen, I became a ski patroller at the same hill as my father, and at age eighteen I moved to Colorado for the sun, skiing, and mountains.

As someone who passionately loves skiing, I suppose no one on earth could have been luckier than me. After my first year of college, during which time I ski patrolled at Eldora Ski Area, I learned that the legendary Berthoud

Pass Ski Area was going to be reopening after having been shuttered for a few years. Berthoud Pass, straddling the continental divide at 11,307' above sea level, was the place of legend. Ski films were shot at Berthoud, early scientific research on avalanches were performed at Berthoud, and it was a mecca for serious skiers. The opportunity to ski patrol at such a place was a once-in-a-lifetime opportunity.

The next three years of ski patrolling at Berthoud Pass were the most consistently exciting and terrifying years of my life. Twice I had to search and then dig through hard packed snow debris to pull out the corpse of a person who met their end under the fury of an avalanche. Twice I myself set off sizeable avalanches – though fortunately in neither case was I carried or buried. I provided emergency care for several skiers who had taken almost unfathomable falls over the massive cliff bands within our ski area boundaries. And I performed CPR for my first time.

Also, during that time, by the skin of my teeth, I survived a fall from nearly the top an icy couloir to the foot of Tyndall Glacier while ski mountaineering in Rocky Mountain National Park. I broke seven bones in the process of that fall and had to miss an entire semester of college while my body and mind slowly healed. And, despite an excellent reconstructive surgeon, some scars from that fall are still visible on my face decades later.

In addition to the thrills and heartaches of those three years, I also began to build so many critical mountain skills. Although I'd never be a truly great skier, there were probably less than a handful of locations in the United States better to learn how to ski tough terrain than at Berthoud Pass. With several local ski movie stars who at the time called Berthoud Pass home, I was lucky enough to ski with (or more accurately, behind) a few of these ski gods. Likewise, suddenly being thrust into such a high avalanche risk environment, my avalanche related skills grew exponentially. My medical skills were continually challenged and improved. And I started to learn the basics of numerous other mountaineering skills – from rock climbing to crevasse rescue – that would serve me well later in life.

My time at Berthoud Pass ended as it was time for graduate school. My lucky streak continued, however, in two ways I would never have foreseen. I left Colorado to go to law school, and when I returned, the Berthoud

Pass Ski Area was again closed, this time for good. With the ski area closed, Berthoud Pass was now a backcountry skiing paradise. Only those willing to ascend under their own power could enjoy this magical place. From my patrol time, I knew Berthoud Pass like the back of my hand, and soon I had written my first book, a guidebook to backcountry skiing at Berthoud Pass.

Likewise, as a young attorney at a large Denver law firm, one of the partners knowing my ski patrol background introduced me to an insurance adjuster for the ski industry. While there are lots of good lawyers who ski, my intimate knowledge of ski area operations from my years as a ski patroller meant that soon a quarter of my law practice would be devoted to defending ski areas in litigation. The ski industry connections I would go on to make as a ski area defense attorney proved to be invaluable.

At about the same time, I started representing ski areas as a young attorney, Heather and I first met. We were neighbors in a high-rise condo in downtown Denver. We quickly became drinking buddies and were drinking buddies for almost a year before we began dating. Once we started dating, we quickly fell in love, and got married near where Heather's parents lived on the Big Island of Hawaii in 2009.

Early on in our relationship, Heather mentioned that we should go on a cruise at some point. At that point in my life, I had no interest in a cruise (as shockingly cruise ships usually do not have skiing) – except for having heard the most incredible stories from a friend who had gone on a cruise in Antarctica. I naturally told Heather that the only way she'd get me on a cruise was if it was in Antarctica. This joke quickly planted the seed of an idea in both our heads. The Antarctica trip came fruition in December 2010.

This Antarctica trip, one of the best trips of our lives, would inspire our subsequent adventures chronicled in this book. There is nothing like visiting Antarctica, the greatest continent on earth. While it provided countless memories, one brief anecdote should provide an overview of the craziness of the continent. On New Years' Eve, as the clock ticked down towards midnight, we were on the makeshift dancefloor of a boat anchored just off the coast of the Antarctic Peninsula. Although just about midnight, the sun was barely below the horizon and it was still, for all intents and purposes, daytime. Consuming vast quantities of pisco sours, we hardly minded the occasional wafting odor of penguin excrement from the shore as we danced. In the never-ending daylight, at midnight, one (and only one) firework was launched from the nearby Chilean research station. And, having agreed to start trying to have kids in 2011, as soon as the countdown to midnight was over, Heather started shouting out: "Babies! Babies! Babies!" We continued to dance in the midnight daylight, celebrating the New Year.

★ ★ ★

And this brings us back to the heroes of this story. In order to ski all seven continents with your kids, besides a healthy sense of adventure and exploration (and patience for endless paperwork), we learned that there are four key things the family needs. Fortunately, we had all four.

First, is skiing ability and knowledge. I was fortunate that my kids loved to ski as much as I did, and that they were both amazing at it for their ages. And it was certainly helpful that from my skiing, mountaineering, and ski patrol background, I knew skiing, mountain travel, avalanche safety, and risk management inside and out.

Second, is the ability to travel. While travelling can be wonderful, let's face it, it can also be quite a chore. Flying overseas involves long plane flights of sitting in small seats for hours on end. It involves battling jet lag and language barriers. While the concept of travel is truly extraordinary – I can wake up in the morning on one continent and go to bed that evening on a different continent – as a practical matter, it has its challenges. And if it is a challenge for adults, it certainly is a challenge for kids. Keira and Maddock were rock stars at travel.

Third, and something I did not realize until we were more than halfway through the continents, is to live in a place where one is lucky enough to ski in great snow conditions all the time. This keeps one from dreading taking ski vacations to just the equivalent of bunny hills in Morocco or in the rainy hills of South Korea. The goal was adventure and experience, not necessarily great (or even decent) skiing, as we fortunately skied enough in the amazing Colorado.

Fourth, and unsurprisingly, is money. Travelling to the six inhabited continents is hardly cheap, and getting down to Antarctic to ski is painfully expensive. Fortunately, Heather and I are both successful professionals, and we would always would rather spend our money on travel than a fancy car or a second home. Or, as people commonly describe it – we spend our money on buying experiences, not things. We are by no means super wealthy, but we're fortunate and lucky enough to have some excess money, and these trips (and of course season passes) are how we chose to spend our money.

The last two items are self-explanatory. The first and second points, however, need more exploration. So, let's spend the next chapter discussing how we instilled a love of skiing, and how this led the kids to be expert skiers at a very young age. After that, spending a chapter on creating children who are expert travelers is equally important. Both chapters will be chock full of the numerous tricks we learned along the way to make travelling and skiing all the continents possible. And for those who are not interested in either topic, feel free to skip ahead by two chapters.

Chapter 2

Skiing North America and How to Ski with Kids (2014 to present)

I have told myself, 'This is how I want to live,' and I do.

Yuichiro Miura

Both kids started skiing as young as practical. Keira's first day was on a small slope near Devil's Thumb Ranch, Colorado in March 2014, two months shy of her second birthday. She was on plastic skis, and I held her the whole time. Maddock's first day, a few months after he turned two, consisted of a few short runs at Berthoud Pass in February 2017 on the same plastic skis as Keira.

Early on I pondered the question of how to make sure my young children would love skiing as much as I do. I remembered a friend of mine had a rule with his kids that they had to eat healthy all the time, except when camping. As he expected, this rule instantly instilled in his kids a love of camping. So, I figured, I could try the same technique.

We made a rule in the house – the only time Keira and Maddock were allowed to have junk food was if we were either skiing, hiking, or camping. We'd hit a convenience store in a gas station before any of those three activities, letting the kids pick out their favorite candies or other junk foods to eat while skiing (or hiking or camping). Unsurprisingly, the kids were quickly begging to go skiing. Even though I looked very silly with my jacket pockets stuffed with candy and chips, it worked like a charm.

But there are more tricks than just bribing the kids with candy. Here are a few of them that I slowly learned:

- I used a four-wheel cart, primarily designed for summer beach use, to pull the kids and their gear from the car to the ski lift. Taking out the uncomfortable walking in ski boots aspect of skiing went a long way to making skiing more pleasant. At the base of the ski lifts, I folded the cart up, locked it to a ski rack with a bike lock, and it was there at the end of the day to haul the kids and gear back.

- I made sure my kids were always warm enough, and also never too warm. As the kids ran colder than me, on cold days I'd purposefully wear fewer clothes myself than I normally would, so I could be more in touch with their temperatures. Skiing is only fun for kids if they are comfortable. And there's no shame in spending time in the lodge.

- We slowly transitioned from candy to other things usually not permitted in our house – such as McDonalds, to accompany ski trips. Lollipops were also a great tool – during longer ski road trips they would get a lollipop every time we went over a pass. And, when Maddock knew how to French Fry (that is, ski with his skis parallel) but still only wanted to Pizza (that is, ski with his skis in a wedge / snowplow), a reward of a lollipop for both him and Keira after every day he predominantly French Fries quickly did the trick of turning him into a skier who only made French Fries (i.e., parallel turns).

- As both a skier and snowboarder, I had the luxury to choose on which gear to teach the kids. While I love both sports (which are really just two facets of the same sport), teaching the kids on skis as opposed to a snowboard first made a huge difference. Being able to separate my own feet made it so much easier to hold, carry, push, pull, lift up, and support the kids at a young age while they learned how to do the same sport as me. At the risk of generating controversy, let me just say it. Between skiing and snowboarding, skiing is the easier one for parents to teach their kids how to do first.

- With season passes that covered multiple ski areas, I would often let the kids decide which ski area on any particular day they wanted to ski. Living in Golden, within two hours we could get to no fewer than a dozen ski areas – A-Basin, Beaver Creek, Breckenridge, Copper, Echo, Eldora, Granby Ranch, Keystone, Loveland, Ski Cooper, Vail, and Winter Park – many of which were included in one of our season passes. By having a voice in where we ski each day, the kids felt they had ownership in the process of the day.

- Similarly, when going to ski areas not within driving distance of our house, I'd consult with the kids about which hotel we wanted to stay at. Their answer was always the same – a hotel with a free breakfast and a pool. Best Western and Holiday Inn Express made lots of money from us over the years, and my kids swam in lots of hotel pools. This helped instill the love of ski trips.

- There are endless games to play while skiing. When driving we would play punch bug – that is, when you see a Volkswagen Beetle, you try to punch the person next to you before they punch you. (It's a light punch, of course.) This game was quickly modified in favor of the kids to my detriment, where they got to punch me, but I couldn't punch back. We adopted this game for the ski slopes – where we played punch onesie. That is, every time the kids saw a person skiing in a one-piece ski suit, they got to punch me. Similarly, we played poke tele – that is, every time they saw a telemark skier (i.e., the type of downhill skiing without a locked heel) they could poke me. As the kids learned from a ski instructor, when riding the lift if they were on chair number one, they could make a wish. Or, if the lift stopped on the tower wheels (or in technical speak, when the grip of our carrier stopped on the sheaves), they could make a wish. Keira and Maddock did everything they could to ride chair one, and always rooted when the lift slowed down just before a tower for it to stop.

- We were always setting goals that kept us skiing. The kids and I loved goals. And I suppose it is obvious that anyone who would try to ski all of the continents has to be a little obsessive about setting creative goals. For example, the kids and I made sure to ski at least one day every month of the year. This is easy to do from October to June while the Colorado ski areas are open. In July and August, we'd be sure to hike up St. Mary's Glacier with me carrying both the kids' and my skis and boots up to the top of the glacier to get in our July and August turns. And in September we'd head down to the Great Sand Dunes National Park to ski on the sand and check off the September month. They anxiously kept track to make sure that they were always getting their ski day in for each month.

Keira and Maddock loved skiing. It wasn't just the food that accompanied it. It was the speed. The challenge. The games. The mastery. The exploration.

And they loved bonding with me over our mutual love of skiing. Most of my favorite things in life – from wine tasting to writing – are not experiences I could share with my young kids. But when it comes to skiing, at least, I could talk with my little kids about all the skiing topics I loved – which are the best ski areas, which are the coolest ski lifts, whether the greatest skier ever was Yuichiro Miura or Shane McConkey, where is the snow the best, which part of the mountain we should explore next, which ski area has the toughest black diamond runs, etc. The list of conversation starters was endless.

While I had quickly accomplished the goal of getting my kids to love skiing – and they soon grew to love it far beyond junk food – that still begged the question of how I personally could stay interested in skiing day after day with the kids while they were still learning. I obviously preferred far more challenging terrain than them. I wasn't about to take them deep in the backcountry through avalanche terrain to go cliff-jumping – as I frequently did with my ski buddies.

Quickly, however, I realized that all our time on comparatively easy terrain would be a great opportunity to really get to know the beginner and intermediate terrain of all the great Colorado ski resorts. As a side benefit, with my law practice partially focused on ski area representation, this would be a wonderful chance to get to visit my connections and get to know their resorts better. And my clients loved that I was visiting their resorts with my young children.

This all meant that it was finally time to accomplish a goal I had long ago set, to ski all 33 ski areas in Colorado. Without the kids, if I was in Aspen, why would I ever ski the relatively easy Buttermilk Ski Area near Aspen, when I could ski the far more challenging Aspen Highlands, or spend a day backcountry skiing near Aspen?

I already knew a litigation expert in my ski cases who was working on this goal of skiing all 33 Colorado ski areas. And I knew a lift engineer who had accomplished this goal as part of his job inspecting ski lifts in Colorado. Otherwise, however, I knew no one who had skied all 33 ski areas in Colorado, or who was even legitimately trying.

With the kids, the goal of finally skiing every ski area in Colorado now sounded like a fun and achievable goal. There were, however, two challenges.

First, there was one ski area in Colorado, Silverton, that had no beginner, intermediate, or even easy advanced terrain. Rather, Silverton's one double chairlift climbed high up on a steep mountain, with not a single child-friendly route down. Further adding to the allure and challenge of Silverton, was the fact that avalanche beacons, shovels, and probes were required to be carried by all skiers. As we began to check-off ski areas, I told both kids the stories about Silverton and its challenges.

As we skied the myriad of other ski areas, we kept in mind that at some point their skills would have to be ready to ski Silverton. Fortunately, each kid was driven to be a strong enough skier to face Silverton's challenges. In addition to skiing constantly with both kids, I spent significant time practicing various steep skiing and deep snow techniques with each of them to get them ready for the rigors of Silverton. Both kids worked amazingly hard on improving their skiing. And we laughed heartily that Keira was too young to read the sign at Aspen Mountain that said, "Experts Only," that she skied underneath on her way to skiing her first double black diamond run. As this story of skiing expert terrain before she could read the word expert became part of our family lore, Maddock learned the spelling of both words, so he recognized the same sign at Taos when he skied his first double black diamond run. Ultimately, Keira skied one run at Silverton at age six in 2019, and Maddock, following in her ski boots once again, also skied one run at Silverton at age six, in 2021.

Second, while many of Colorado's great ski areas are a short drive from Golden, many others are a long drive. So, to ski all 33 ski areas in the state, the kids would have to be okay piling into my Subaru, prepared to drive 8 hours to ski. Although the idea had yet to strike Heather and me to have them try to break a world record of being the youngest person to ski all the continents, working on the goal of skiing all 33 ski areas in Colorado depended upon their patience for travel, albeit just road travel as opposed to road, sea, and air travel.

Indeed, by the time Keira ultimately broke the world record of the youngest person to ski on all seven continents, in the United States alone she had skied at over fifty different ski areas in Alaska, California, Colorado, New Mexico, and Utah.

Before delving into how we decided to embark on the quest that is the focus of this book, it's worth discussing how we ended up with two kids who are so good at travelling.

Keira and Maddock exhausted after a day of skiing

Keira and Maddock skiing the cirque at Winter Park, Colorado

Keira skiing at age 3

Chapter 3

Travelling the World with Children (2016 to present)

I have travelled the world to ski, to soar with the winds, and to laugh with the gods.

Yuichiro Miura

I f you want to ski at the ends of the earth, you have to be patient with travel. By way of example, to ski in the Snowy Mountains of Australia coming from Colorado, it's a few hours flight from Denver to Los Angeles, a 14 plus hour flight from Los Angeles to Sydney, Australia, and a six plus hour drive from Sydney to the Australian ski areas. That's a lot of travel for an adult. How would young kids be patient with that sort of travel?

We initially did not plan to take large international trips with the kids when they were very young. After all, shortly before Keira turned one, I was stuck travelling alone with her on an airplane flight from New York to Denver. It was an awful experience. Perhaps the worst moment was shortly before boarding while Keira was crying, a lady I did not know came up to me and comically tried womansplaining to me how I should check Keira's diaper, make sure she had food, etc. – advice that even the most inexperienced father would know. In any event, between crying, diapers, and temper tantrums throughout the whole flight experience, I swore to Keira that we'd never travel alone again until she turned eighteen. (I obviously did not keep that promise for very long.) Travelling with toddlers is not easy.

Our decision to begin taking big overseas trips with our kids at a young age was the result a reason far different than for most parents who are aggressive travelers. My father was eighty-seven when Maddock was born. Although he was in great health – for example, he was still skiing when Keira learned to ski – from a purely statistical standpoint his age made it more likely that he'd pass away when Keira and Maddock were young than any of their other three grandparents. If this was to happen, God forbid, Heather and I wanted to make sure the kids remembered him. Besides being a genuinely good person and loving parent and grandparent, he was perhaps the most interesting person in an interesting family. He had been a research engineer who had twenty patents on new inventions. He was likewise a passionate adventurer who at various times in his life skied, biked, rode horses, hunted, and flew planes. He was still fluent in Italian into his seventies based upon the extended time he had lived in Italy studying sculpture before I was born.

My father was (and is) a memorable person, but the kids were young. So just in case he did not live much longer, we pondered how to make sure the kids would remember him. Considering the issue, Heather pointed out that the one thing both of us remembered when we were very young was travel. So, we decided to do at least one large international trip with my parents each year. How better for the kids to keep memories of him? We proposed an international trip to my parents without telling them the morbid reason. We gave them the choice of where to go for our first trip, and they chose Switzerland in the summer.

Before the Switzerland trip, I was having drinks with a work colleague with little kids, whose parents lived in Southeast Asia. Fearing the upcoming Switzerland trip, and seeking advice, I asked him how he and his wife were able to travel half-way across the world with little kids to visit his parents.

He asked, "don't you know about the *travel fairy?*" With only those few words, I knew I was about to hear a brilliant idea. He explained to me that the *travel fairy* travels through the overhead bins in airplanes, spying on the children. She leaves presents in the carry-on bags for the well-behaved children, but she leaves nothing for the naughty children. After telling Keira and Maddock about the *travel fairy*, we had two wonderfully well-behaved children on their first international flight, and we found lots of little wrapped presents in our carry-on luggage. And as a bonus, they had new toys to play with on the flight.

The summer Switzerland trip taught us that it wasn't too hard to travel internationally with the kids. Soon, our kids were accomplished travelers. They were always excited to board the airplane to fly to exotic locations, and equally excited to hop in the car for long road trips.

Our kids quickly just got used to travelling. When they were younger, they loved having the lollipops during take-off and landing so the changing air pressure in the cabin wouldn't bother their ears. They loved having us check for *travel fairy* presents. And they were always more patient than we were with flight delays and the other headaches of travel. This is not to mention that every airport naturally presented itself as a giant playground to explore.

We soon learned two other tricks. First, separating the kids was always best. We were more attentive parents if it's one on one as opposed to two on two. Further, keeping the kids in different rows meant that they were not able to fight with each other.

Second, they each got mini-iPads with videos and games to watch. As we strictly limited television and video games at home, airplane travel was a special event for them.

As they got older, lollipops and the *travel fairy* were no longer necessary, but at this point the lessons had been learned. The kids were expert travelers.

Heather and I learned tricks not only for the travel time, but also to prepare them for the time in the foreign countries. We needed to figure out what the local food was that they would like, and also what the local food was that they would at least tolerate. So, multiple trips to restaurants in the Denver metro-area with similar food to the location was key. And there's nothing like building a Lego set of the location – and our shelf above the fireplace as well as shelves in the kids' rooms are now littered with Lego versions of the Sydney Opera House, the London Skyline (for our layover time getting to the Atlas Mountains of Morocco), and many other locales.

As an aside, as a portion of this book discusses parenting, I find it rather odd that I'm writing a book partly on parenting. I feel as if I'm never very good at it. Everyone tells me I'm a great dad, but being a dad seems really difficult. It was particularly difficult when the kids were babies and toddlers.

I always tell my friends with babies and toddlers to be patient, because it does get better. It was on a ski trip when I finally realized life as a parent had started to get easier. With Heather headed to Italy for a week of work in late May 2018 (roughly six months before we skied in Italy to start checking off new continents), and not sure what else to do, I booked a trip with my kids to what was then called Squaw Valley, California, now called Palisades Tahoe. Keira and Maddock were five and three.

Had we not prepaid for everything, while packing the night before our travels, I might have just thrown in the towel and not done the trip. Travelling alone with two young kids (flight, rental car, condo, etc.) sounded so daunting. But, despite my reservations, the trip worked perfectly – and I realized if I could fly across the western states with the kids lugging ski gear, rent a car, and ski at one of the legendary ski resorts – parenting had definitely gotten easier. And the kids were well on their way to being better – or at least cheerier – travelers than my wife and me.

With kids who were quickly becoming as good at travel as they were at skiing, the only thing left to beginning the quest to break the world record was the idea. That would come soon.

Chapter 4

The Genesis of the Idea (December 2018)

It will be the end when people lose heart and stop looking for new and challenging problems.
Yuichiro Miura (paraphrasing Sir Edmund Hillary)

A s Christmas vacation of 2018 approached, Heather and I debated where to take the family. At the time, she was working for an Italian company, and she thought it would be good for her to continue working on learning basic Italian. I wanted to go skiing (of course). Heather was no longer skiing, owing to a broken leg from skiing years earlier that had turned her off from the sport. But she still loved the apres-ski portion of the sport. After all, apres-ski is an important aspect of skiing.

So, it didn't take long for us to decide that the perfect vacation would be the Italian Alps. It met Heather's Italian practice goal and my skiing goal. Plus, having skied previously in Switzerland, and spent time wine tasting in Italy, I knew that I'd much prefer a week of eating Italian food than eating Swiss food. (Sorry Switzerland!)

So, we booked a trip to Cervinia, high in the Italian Alps. Americans tend to know the name Zermatt, Switzerland much better than Cervinia, Italy, but they are one and the same resort. There are two different towns – one on the Swiss side (Zermatt) and one on the Italian side (Cervinia), that each access the same gigantic cross-border ski area. And both towns lie below different faces of the imposing Matterhorn. Just to keep things confusing, the Swiss, German, and English-speaking peoples refer to the mountain as the Matterhorn, while the Italians refer to the same mountain as Cervino. As if two names were not confusing enough already for this majestic mountain, there is a third name as well. Although the Matterhorn straddles the Swiss / Italian border, as it's only twenty miles to the French border, the French have their own name for the Matterhorn: Cervin.

The thought of skiing all the continents had never been in my mind two months before this Italian ski trip. From Heather and my trip to Antarctica pre-kids, which was not a ski trip, I had gazed lustfully at the amazing ski lines on the Antarctic Peninsula. I definitely wanted to return someday to Antarctica with my skis. But otherwise, I never even considered skiing all the continents.

The inspiration to ski all the continents came from the most unlikely of sources. As an avid reader, I was slowly making my way through the myriad of books written by the great Winston Churchill. While reading his book, *The Grand Alliance*, in his usual beautiful prose, Churchill referenced the snowcapped Atlas Mountains above Marrakech, Morocco during his meetings with Franklin Roosevelt in Marrakech. I Googled the Atlas Mountains, and I was shocked to see a series of peaks that looked like the Colorado Rockies. A second quick web search revealed that there was decent backcountry skiing in the Atlas Mountains.

I thought of how cool it would be to actually ski in Africa. Then I thought about the fact that I had always wanted to ski in Antarctica. I knew there was skiing on the other continents – in fact I had a good friend in Sydney, Australia – my counterpart who was a lawyer who represented the Australian ski areas. I had always told him one day I'd visit Australia and ski with him in his country, like he had skied with me in the United States many times. The idea of skiing on all seven continents gradually began to take shape in my head.

The concept of skiing all seven continents, slowly festering and growing in my head, was at the beginning an idea I only had for myself. I wanted to ski the seven continents. It was about me. It wasn't until a month or two later, as we were about to fly to Italy, that the thought of bringing the kids along to ski all the continents first entered my head.

As I would joke several years later – as we closed in on completing the quest and our travels were starting to get covered in the media – my initial idea had been for me to do this for myself. But, had I gone to Heather with the suggestion that I was going to take the time and expense to ski all of the continents, she would have emphatically responded no. It would be way too expensive and way too much time away from home. Then I got the brilliant idea that the way to talk her into this was to turn it into a family adventure. Once it became a goal for the kids and me to accomplish skiing the seven continents together to chase a record (with her on all or at least most of the trips) – suddenly I went from being the world's most selfish husband to the world's greatest dad. We were bringing the kids to the most exotic locales, and all of us were learning about the world together.

Two quick asides. First, I'm a pretty smart husband. Second, in case it was not already obvious, I am also the luckiest person in the world.

So how to reach this crazy goal with kids? Much like the fun and far easier goal of skiing every ski area in Colorado, that we were already working on, I knew that we had to start by just checking places off the list. Start with the easy ones and save the more challenging locations for down the road.

Five of the seven continents are for all intents and purposes easy to ski. Of course, this depends upon having children who are both good travelers and good skiers, and likewise having enough money, determination, and grit for the travel and skiing. We had already skied North America, our home continent, and we were about to check-off Europe. South America has numerous ski areas in the Andes, and I knew that there were ski areas close to Santiago, Chile. Santiago was a relatively accessible location – a flight from Denver with only a single connection in Houston (mind you, we fly only on United Airlines if we can). Australia has ski areas sandwiched between Sydney and Melbourne. Several Asian countries have ski areas. So, without any research, I knew five of the seven continents wouldn't be an issue other than the time and money commitment. And with my extensive background in skiing – as a ski patroller, backcountry skier, guidebook author, and avalanche safety instructor – I knew the ins and outs of safe skiing pretty much anywhere.

That just left two challenging continents – Africa and Antarctica. A quick Google search revealed that there were actually a few ski areas in Morocco, although tiny by American or European standards. So, if we could pull off the exotic Morocco; then there was just the question of backcountry skiing Antarctica.

Antarctica doesn't have any ski areas. But it has plentiful backcountry options (i.e., skiing without a ski lift, where you climb or skin up, and then ski down). Being an avid backcountry skier with a laundry list of qualifications in the field, this would be no major challenge for me. But what about the kids? I figured we should just leave the challenging continents for the last ones to do and concentrate on the easy ones first.

Curious if there was a world record for the youngest person, a quick web search showed it was a fellow American, Victoria Rae White. She broke the record in 2008 at the age of 10 years and 79 days. (The accomplishment of Victoria and her parents will reenter this story later.) So, now we knew that this was a record worthy of the Guinness Book of World Records, and we knew the deadline to break the record.

During the flight from Denver to Newark on the way to ski the Italian Alps with the family, I sketched out a plan on a sheet of paper that figured a ski trip on a new continent every six months would get Keira (then six-year-old) in well under the record. If we could double up Africa with another continent in one six-month period, then Keira would be a little younger than nine when we accomplished the goal. Figuring one or two trips we'd have to redo; we'd have over a year and a half buffer space for Keira. If she was up for Antarctica (and perhaps Maddock as well), this could work.

And it hardly seemed fair to Keira that if she was doing all the skiing with her younger brother, that she would never hold the record if Maddock completed all of them at the same time. So, we'd plan for one continent just with Keira and me, so she could break the record first. Then, we'd check off that continent with Maddock (then four-year-old) down the road, so he could then break Keira's record and hold the record himself.

While Heather and I loved the plan, neither of us thought we'd actually pull it off. But to paraphrase Ralph Waldo Emerson (or Aerosmith, if you prefer), what's important is the journey, not the destination. There's so much of the world we could see and experience as we tried for the record that we wouldn't experience otherwise. So, why not at least give it a shot?

Considering that it was unlikely we'd actually pull it off, both Heather and I agreed not to tell anyone (other than the kids and my parents) about the plan. And this especially made sense for another reason as well. I knew lots of dedicated skiers in Colorado, both in and out of the ski industry, who have professional jobs and young children. I hated the idea that if we told everyone about our plans, the word would get passed along, and someone would swoop in and break the record before our kids got the chance. So, without telling anyone why we were about to start skiing in random spots all over the world, we started to make the plans.

We also discussed making sure that it was fun for the kids, and not a burden. We wanted to get their buy-in, which we received quickly and enthusiastically. They loved the idea as much as we did. And Heather and I agreed that if at any time they weren't still having fun, we would stop trying to chase this crazy idea.

Succeed or fail, this goal would let us discover all sorts of new places. We'd see places we'd never expect to go and learn so much more about the world. The plan would happily force us to travel more, and travel to more exotic locales. Indeed, Heather and I had only been to five of the seven continents when we came up with the idea. What a better way to get us to see all the continents.

The idea of chasing a world record seemed simultaneously both cool and bizarre. I love staring out the windows of airplanes, and I am perpetually blown away when close to landing how many countless houses there are. Each house has a family – with their adventures, stories, triumphs, and tragedies. And to think that it is possible for even one brief moment to do something no one in any of those hundreds of millions of houses has ever done sounded pretty amazing. It also sounds pretty outlandish.

Let me break the temporal sequence briefly to fast forward in time. When I came up with the idea, I did not realize how truly bizarre going after a record would be. As I would later learn, chasing a world record is inherently lonely. We could not talk to anyone about how to do it. While we knew a person here or there who had skied in some obscure place or another where we were headed, no one could give us a roadmap on how to do this. In spite of my seemingly endless ski connections, I knew of no one who had skied all the crazy places we were planning. And of course, no one could tell us how to accomplish the goal with kids in tow.

I also did not anticipate at the time how challenging the record-chase would be. It should have been self-explanatory that breaking a world record, no matter how obscure or silly, would be very difficult. There's a reason why it's a world record. At the beginning, we thought we were just in for a lot of travel (with its usual headaches of jet lag and custom lines) and a lot of skiing (which I could train the kids to do). However, we were to face cancelled trip after cancelled trip. We were to get rejection after rejection in attempts to get to Antarctica with both kids and skis. We had the never-ending threat of weather – sometimes not enough snow, other times too much snow. And this is not to mention the broken car, the quarantine, the foreign language paperwork, etc. The hurdles would someday feel endless.

Years after we came up with the plan, and after what seemed like the hundredth setback, with the clock ticking down on the deadline to break the world record, over a bottle of wine, I vented my frustrations to Heather on the seemingly never-ending setbacks. Heather reassured me that we were doing our best to accomplish the goal. In this conversation and thinking through the issues, I found some solace in the old JFK quote: we do these things "not because they are easy, but because they are hard." This process was not easy. I repeatedly just wished that breaking a world record would be easy. The process was fun, fascinating, and frustrating, but it was not easy. How naïve of me to think otherwise as our plans first took shape.

Regardless, we had a plan. And our adventures were about to begin.

PART 2

THE NEXT FOUR CONTINENTS – EUROPE, AUSTRALIA, ASIA, AND AFRICA

Chapter 5

Skiing Europe (January 2019)

And this gray spirit, yearning in desire to follow knowledge.

Alfred Lord Tennyson

Among the dumbest things I've ever done in my entire life, and I've done many dumb things (two of them are recounted in this book), was the night before we were to head to our second continent. I forgot that my passport was in a back pocket of my jeans, which I laundered so I'd have more clean clothes for travel. Realizing my blunder and flipping through my tattered passport, I was in a complete panic that customs would not accept it. Despite the pit in my stomach of dread each time I pulled out my passport, no one seemed to blink an eye at my water-logged passport in customs. Before we knew it, we were in the Italian Alps.

Although I had not previously been to the Italian Alps, as I had skied in the Swiss Alps and had spent time travelling around Italy, this trip would be the least foreign of any of the continents that I did not call home. And, at this point the idea of skiing all the continents was just a crazy idea I had come up with and had outlined by hand on a single sheet of paper. We weren't heading to ski in Italy for the purposes of breaking the world record. Rather, we were headed there for a pre-planned ski vacation.

Heather and I wanted to have a separate room from the kids for the week in Italy, and pretty soon it became obvious that the best deal was a Club Med in Cervinia. We had never been to a Club Med before, but any hotel that offers kids programs sounded amazing to us. For our first few full days at Cervinia, we put the kids in the Club Med's ski school. I decided to spend two days with the free Club Med adult ski school before spending a day in the backcountry, and then spending one day skiing with each kid in turn, and finally one day skiing with both kids.

This trip was the only one during our adventures that I skied more on my own than with the kids. In retrospect, this trip almost seemed out of place compared to the other ones. So, unlike future chapters that recount family stories, this chapter is filled almost solely with my own anecdotes and observations on culture, skiing, and the intersection of the two.

For our first full day after arrival, the kids went into the Club Med kids ski school, and I joined up with the Club Med adult ski school for a tour of the mountain and to meet some folks. While our instructor was Italian, the group consisted of skiers from all over Europe and one person from overseas: me. Happily, the common language of the group (as it always seems to be) was English.

I was relieved that the common language was English as unfortunately that is the only language I speak. As I travel a lot, I jokingly say that after a few days in German or Italian speaking areas, I can speak "bar German" or "bar Italian." That means that with my broken German or Italian, I can go to a noisy bar, order drinks, and pay in German or Italian. However, if the bar is quiet so they can hear my atrocious pronunciation, or if anything goes wrong in the process like the bartender asking me a question not about drinks or paying, then my German or Italian will fail me. My French pronunciation is even worse, but my vocabulary is a bit larger. So, I always say after a few days of practice, I can speak "restaurant French." This means that after a few days in a French speaking area, I can get a table, order food and wine, and pay. But again, nothing can go wrong, and the locals will be horrified with my pronunciation. Years ago in France, I remember asking in French for a wine list. The waiter responded in French that (as I later learned) they didn't have a wine list, but rather one had to walk down to their wine cellar and pick out the bottle. That's what I mean by things going wrong – anything unusual and my very limited French would fail me. Fortunately, between my lousy pronunciation and the amazing ability of most people to speak English, any conversation could usually revert to English.

My Spanish skills (or more accurately my lack of Spanish skills) will be discussed in more depth in later chapters when we were in the Andes and Patagonia.

Throughout my first day skiing in the Club Med ski school group, each person in the group asked me where I lived in the United States or Canada. (It was my clothes that instantly gave away that I wasn't European, which I'll explain in a minute.) I already knew how the conversation would go from the prior times I had skied in the Alps. I'd respond that I was from Colorado, and the first words out of their mouths always were: "what are you doing skiing here?"

Colorado deservedly has the reputation as one of the greatest ski spots in the world – we have lots of snow, the snow itself is some of the lightest in the world, and we have great mountains. In many ski circles, this means that if one lives in Colorado (or Utah), one should never leave there to ski elsewhere. While I love Colorado, I disagree with this attitude. Skiing in the Alps is an incredible experience that shouldn't be missed.

For those Americans who have never skied in the Alps before, it's worth a brief description for comparison's sake. While Colorado and Utah on average have better snow than the Alps, our mountains are neither as spectacular nor as big. Skiing in the Alps is just on a grander scale than skiing in North America.

Perhaps more important is that the entire culture is more skiing focused. The small country of Austria boasts almost the same number of skier visit days per year as the entire United States. Talk about a ski culture! And the biggest ski area in the world, Les 3 Vallees, France, has more ski lifts than every Colorado ski area put together. Indeed, in www.skiresort.info's ranking of ski areas by size, the 10 biggest ski resorts in the world are all located in the Alps. In my day job as an attorney who represents American ski resorts, I've gotten the opportunity to know a number of ski lift engineers. One of these engineers once explained to me – that many years ago there was a war between the European and American ski lift manufacturers on who could make the bigger and better lifts. The Europeans won. And we lost. At Cervinia / Zermatt, this was very apparent. It seemed as if three-quarters of the ski lifts were (what we today consider to be the top-of-the-line) six-pack bubble chair lifts.

Although the Cervinia ski lift system was state-of-the-art, the lift lines were a mess. As far as I could tell, this appeared to be not a result of the lifts or the number of skiers, but rather the diversity of languages. There was no common language for the lift operators to use to get folks to queue up into groups of six properly. English, French, German, Italian, and Russian were ubiquitous in the lift lines – with at least a dozen of other languages being spoken by the various skiers.

Not only were the ski lifts more top-of-the-line than in the United States, the ski area of Zermatt / Cervinia itself is gigantic. If I'm skiing aggressively, while perhaps I cannot ride every lift at Colorado's biggest ski area, Vail, in one day, I can take at least one run on virtually every part of the mountain. At Cervinia / Zermatt, however, the ski area was so large it would take a few days to get to every part of the mountain, and at least a week to ride every lift. The scale of the ski area was much larger than in America.

Another difference between American and European skiing is the relative height of treeline. Treeline is the top elevation at a given location in which trees can survive and grow. Trees stop growing above a certain altitude – and the biggest factor for determining that altitude by location is the summertime temperatures. As such, if you only visit ski areas in the winter, by Colorado standards Vermont seems to have a very high treeline and the Alps seem to have a very low treeline. Not a single ski area in Vermont has above treeline skiing. Many Colorado resorts have above treeline skiing, but the vast majority of Colorado terrain is below treeline. But in the Alps, the vast majority of the ski terrain is above treeline, often far above treeline. The summers in the Alps are comparatively cold – resulting in more pristine high alpine terrain in the winters. The opposite is true in Vermont.

The comparatively low treeline in the Alps makes for some odd sights. Cervinia / Zermatt has snowmaking machines from the bottom to far above treeline. Snowmaking machines high above treeline are all but nonexistent in the United States. While snowmaking is ubiquitous at lower elevations in Colorado, it is all but absent at the higher elevations, such as above treeline. The snowmaking machines in the high alpine environments in the Alps are both a result of a lower treeline relative to winter weather and the fact that global warming has hit the Alps far worse than it has hit the Rockies so far. (Several years later, I would notice the same things in the Andes as we skied South America.)

With wide expanses of terrain above treeline, one would think people in Europe would ski everywhere. In spite of the gigantic skiable terrain above treeline, however, very little of it actually gets skied. European skiing involves the concept of *pistes*, for which there is no direct translation into American English. Literally, *piste* translates to either the word "track" or "trail," but that hardly conveys the difference in views of how ski area terrain is skied. Let me explain the concept.

In the United States and Canada, ski areas have many runs under each lift. Below treeline, these runs are separated by trees. Typically, but not universally, in North America the treed terrain between runs is considered to be part of the ski area, though only to be accessed from marked locations. Above treeline, typically, most terrain is open to ski and part of the ski area unless designated as closed or off-limits terrain. In the United States and Canada, the outer boundary of the resort is typically marked (in a variety of ways), and closed areas within the boundaries are also marked. Beyond the boundary is backcountry – uncontrolled and not patrolled – but within the boundary is the ski area. And, in North America, of the runs/trails themselves, some are groomed and some are not, the latter allowing for more powder and more bumps on ski runs.

The Europeans have a very different view of terrain. Each ski lift accesses only one or two *pistes*, typically marked on both sides by flags. The *pistes* are groomed, but nothing else is groomed. If you're skiing on the *piste*, you're skiing *on-piste*. If you're not skiing on the *piste*, you're skiing *off-piste* and you're on your own so to speak, even if you're directly under a ski lift. Avalanche control work is only done on *off-piste* terrain if the avalanche could run onto a *piste*. Otherwise, if you leave the *piste*, you're now into entirely unpatrolled and uncontrolled areas. It's a very different approach to ski terrain than our approach in North America.

I had the fun of discussing the various differences between the Alps and the Rockies with the group of fellow hotel guests and the instructor with whom I was skiing. Although I made some of the above points, they pointed out several differences between our respective skiing homes that I had missed. First, they were amused by my clothing. My ski clothes neither matched nor were in good shape. They were even more amused by my ski poles (which I had bought at a rental shop in Girdwood Alaska many years earlier for $10). My ski poles didn't have matching grips, didn't have matching baskets, and looked at least 30 years old. As more than one European explained to me, my clothing and gear screamed out that I was an American.

As they explained to me, rich Europeans tend to flaunt their wealth while Americans seem embarrassed by their wealth. From a cultural standpoint, Europe is more class based and America is more egalitarian. There are no barons, dukes, or lords in America. I must be wealthy, they reasoned, as I was able to afford a week-long ski trip with my family in Cervinia. Any European who has sufficient funds to fly to a fancy ski resort for a week of skiing with his or her family would never be seen out on the slopes with the old and rundown gear I had. They almost seemed wistful for a society with less pressure to show off your relative wealth.

While my clothing and equipment's condition stood out the most to announce me as American, our conversations on gondola rides may have given the Europeans false impressions that all Americans were like me. We jokingly went through my ski pant pockets, which they (unfairly) considered to be stereotypical American. I showed them how I always had a Swiss Army Knife on me – as one never knows when one might randomly need a screwdriver, knife, or corkscrew. Here, right next to Switzerland, only the American religiously carried a Swiss Army Knife. And the Europeans got a good chuckle how I carry caffeine pills in case I ever get sleepy and can't access coffee. For better or worse, probably worse, they assumed that my knife and caffeine pills reflected all Americans. (Thank goodness I don't ski with a handgun!)

The European skiers who had skied in Colorado (and there were quite a few) also pointed out that they were terrified in Colorado that Americans often didn't lower the restraint bars on their chairlifts. (I personally always lower the restraint bar.) They could not understand how America is such an overly safety conscious country, with seat belts, ski helmets, and lawsuits galore, yet most Colorado skiers do not lower their chairlift restraint bars. I laughed, tried to explain the science, and the myriad of pros and cons of restraint bars — yet the idea to them of not lowering a restraint bar was utterly foreign. No pun intended.

The last major difference between skiing in the Alps versus in America, is how much more of a drinking culture the Europeans have. No one batted an eyebrow at someone drinking a bottle of wine over lunch while skiing. Indeed, I remembered from years earlier skiing in Switzerland on my own and going to a bar around 3 pm every afternoon that was about two-thirds of the way down the ski area. I'd drink heavily, along with all the other tourists and locals, until ski patrol showed up about 4:30 pm to make an announcement in German. While I don't speak German, my vague understanding was that the ski patrol announcement was that they were doing the sweep of the mountain, and we all better get our last drinks, pay our bill, and head down before it got dark. The other patrons and I would finish our drinks, stammer out of the bar, and loopily put on our skis and boards. We'd then proceed to ski down the mountain in the growing darkness, drunk, and happy.

The European drinking culture is inexorably intertwined with the European food culture. As one would expect, the on-the-mountain dining in Cervinia was excellent. As the ski area straddles the Swiss and Italian borders, on days when one could cross from side-to-side, you could practically see the swarms of skiers coming over to the Italian side for lunch, and then returning to the Swiss side afterwards. While there are certainly fun Swiss dishes, Italian food ranks among the best in the world, and there's nothing like eating great Italian food in Italy between ski runs.

In sum, while the ski conditions on average are superior in Colorado, the ski culture on average is better in Europe.

The kids had fun in ski school (though Keira and Maddock later claimed they did not like it at all as they were not skiing with me). Beyond getting a backcountry day in for myself, I made sure to ski with each kid separately for one day. Perhaps the funniest moment when I was skiing just with Keira occurred on a lift ride shared with four others who spent the whole ride speaking in a foreign language. Keira was complaining that I wasn't letting her ski any black diamonds. (Owing to the very icy conditions, I didn't feel that her skiing the few steep open runs was appropriate that day.) After her complaining for half the lift ride of "all I want is to ski a black diamond run," I mocked her by mimicking her voice and tone, saying "all I want is a daughter who doesn't complain." The four others on the lift burst into laughter at my impression of her – a good reminder that while I understood not a word of their language, they sure could understand me.

Perhaps the funniest moment with Maddock while just the two of us were skiing together occurred lower on the mountain. Maddock had had several days in a row of skiing in ski school, and he was used to the fact that in ski school when his group was snaking down the mountain with each kid following the one in front, that he should follow the kid in front of him. So, on our day skiing together, when he saw a group of ski school kids all following their instructor down the mountain, he promptly fell into line at the tail end following them down the mountain. I had to call out to him to remind him that he was skiing with me, not this random ski school group.

On the last day, Keira, Maddock, and I all skied together. Then, it was time to head home, with a quick stop in the Lake Country to see a place to which we had never been. The hotel in the Lake Country called us while in Cervinia to confirm we were still coming – which made sense when we found out on our arrival that we were the only guests staying in the large hotel that evening. The Lake Country, we learned, was a summer and not winter tourist attraction. But the soaring Alps above the placid lakes provided amazing scenery, regardless of the time of year.

I cannot wait to return to ski the Alps again. While it is by no means perfect, it is a great place. But the land down under was calling our names.

Keira riding the tram at Cervinia, Italy

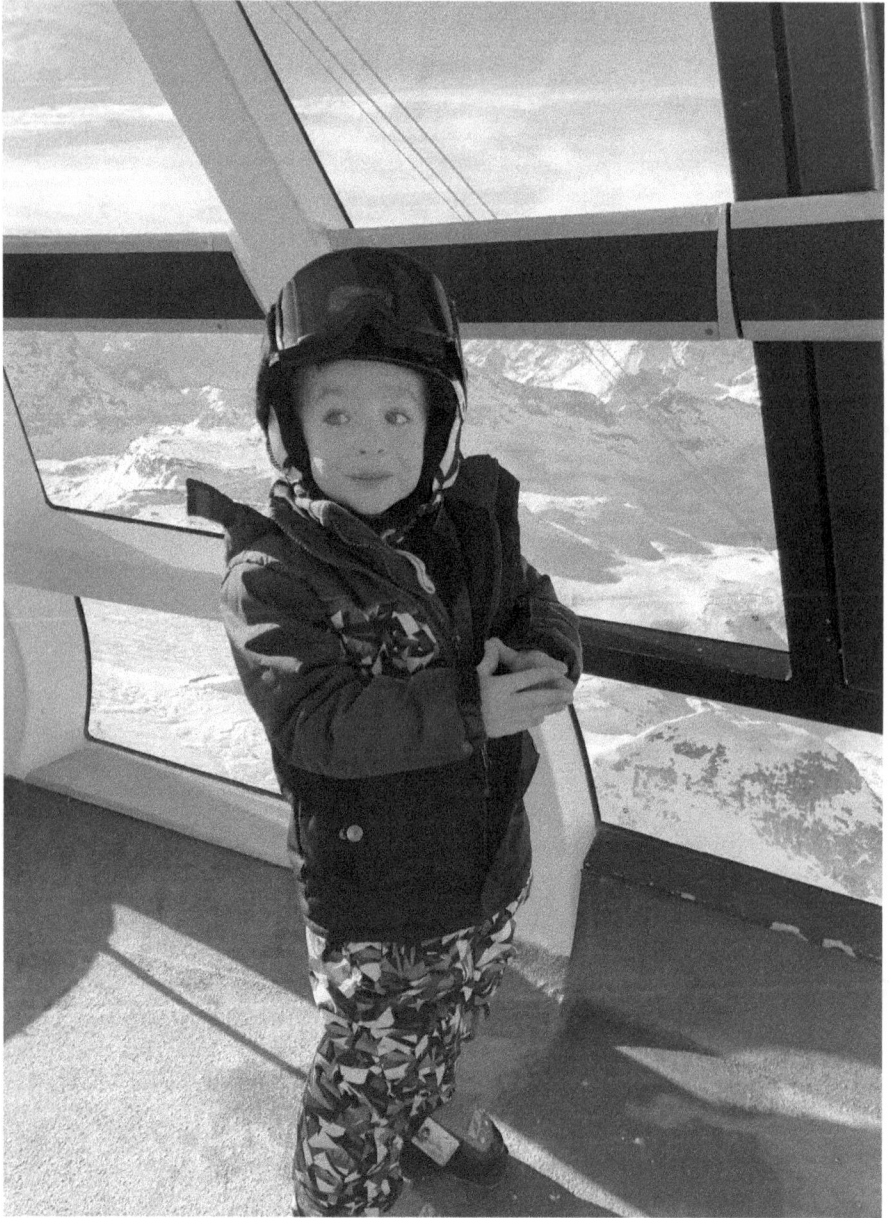

Maddock riding the tram at Cervinia, Italy

Chapter 6

Skiing Australia (July 2019)

Much have I seen and known.

Alfred Lord Tennyson

Unlike a trip to the Alps, that could be completely focused around skiing, it hardly made sense to focus an entire trip to Australia around skiing. For starters, none of us had been to Australia, and Heather and I wanted to see more of it. Moreover, Australia's Snowy Mountains are hardly the Alps or the Rockies, so why focus an entire trip on skiing? So, we decided to spend a week in Sydney, and then I'd drive down to the Snowy Mountains with the kids while lucky Heather flew to Adelaide to spend a day wine tasting in the Barossa Valley and the next day wine tasting in McLaren Vale.

So, we were off on our next adventure. Having already bought and assembled the Lego Sydney Opera House, the kids were thrilled to see the real Sydney Opera House. We had a fun week in Sydney of sight-seeing. And my wife and I were able to catch up with my Australian counterpart and good friend – an attorney who worked with the Australian ski resorts. After a week in Sydney, Heather flew off to Adelaide for her wine tasting adventures. I rented a large SUV, and the kids and I headed down towards Australia's Snowy Mountains.

This was my first time driving on the opposite side of the road, or as I am prone to say, the wrong side of the road. Needless to say, I was nervous. Keira and Maddock, from the back seat, gleefully counted up every time I turned on my windshield wipers – as opposed to my turn signal – by accident. Considering the length of the drive to the Snowy Mountains, the time we spent in the Snowy Mountains, and my comparative unfamiliarity of driving on the opposite side of the road – they had lots of times to laugh at the windshield wipers going on with clear skies.

While I had always read how empty Australia was – it is basically the same size as the continuous United States (i.e., the lower 48) with a total population less than California – the vast expanse of unpopulated lands only came into perspective as we drove to the Snowy Mountains. The distance between each town was enormous. The few towns we passed were small. And in between them lay no people, only kangaroos. Having driven many times through Wyoming, the least populated state in the United States, the countryside of Australia seemed even more sparsely populated.

We rented skis along the way to the Snowy Mountains. When the Australians asked us where we were from after hearing my very non-Australian accent, I told them Colorado. And, at the rental shop (and the ski areas) I heard the same refrain as in the Alps. "If you're from Colorado, why are you skiing here?" I explained to the Australians that it was summertime in Colorado, and that seemed to satisfy everyone who asked. The rental store employees warned me to watch out for kangaroos on the road as dusk approached, and to watch out for wallabies running across the ski slopes when I was on the mountain. These warnings just made me more excited for the adventure.

We stayed at the base of the Snowy Mountains in a cabin at an RV Park location that was perfect for Keira and Maddock. The location had a bouncy device in the playground somewhat like a trampoline, which they loved. Keira described it as a bouncy house without walls or a ceiling. The town we were staying in, Jindabyne, was at the fork in the road dividing up the two biggest ski areas in New South Wales – Perisher and Thredbo – and our cabin was just by this junction.

The next day we went to Perisher – the largest ski area by some accounts anywhere south of the equator. And it's on the Epic Pass. We rode Perisher's 8 passenger chairlift, the first time I had ever been on a chairlift carrying so many people. We skied all around the maze of lifts (the ski area is a large conglomeration of several ski areas connected by lifts and an underground train). The snow reminded me of East Coast snow. We stuck around for a little night skiing to watch fireworks. As the kids got cold, waiting for the fireworks, we went into an open bar. Considering how terrified I am to drive on the opposite side of the road, I opted for a hot chocolate at the bar, just like the kids, not wanting even a sip of alcohol. As we sat in the bar drinking our hot cocoa, the musician playing guitar sang Men at Work's "Land Down Under." It was almost too perfect, hearing a cover of the classic song Americans associate with Australia, while sipping hot cocoa in ski boots, in the Snowy Mountains of Australia.

Once back in Jindabyne that evening, the only restaurant within walking distance of the cabin (and after a day of driving on the wrong side of the road, I really wanted a drink) was a Thai restaurant. I ordered all the kid-friendly Thai food, such as Pad Thai, but was surprised to see that Keira wanted none of it. If it wasn't pizza or cheeseburgers, she simply didn't want to eat it. Well, this could make skiing in Asia a bit of a culinary challenge for us. I knew my wife and I would have our work cut out for us convincing Keira that there's good food beyond pizza and cheeseburgers.

The next day we went to Thredbo. While Perisher was much wider than Thredbo, Thredbo was much taller. Thredbo is on the Ikon Pass, and I felt right at home with the two biggest ski areas in the region each being on one of the major American ski season passes. At Thredbo, the kids were excited, instead of exploring, to just loop the same lift (with a small feature terrain park) over and over again.

After two fun days of skiing, the next morning we packed up our stuff into our SUV and started the six-hour drive back to Sydney. It had been a fun trip, and our flight back to the United States was scheduled to leave the next morning from the Sydney airport.

With my gas tank a third full, I put in $20 of regular gas before leaving Jindabyne. (I figured that I'd top it off once I reached the less expensive gas stations in the slightly larger town of Cooma on the drive back to Sydney.) We began driving north towards Sydney. On every hill we climbed up between Jindabyne and Cooma, the SUV's engine would start knocking. How odd, I thought. I knew what engine knocking was, but I wasn't sure I had ever heard it before. And once in Cooma, we stopped first at the McDonalds and it took four attempts to get the car to start. I suspected the car needed higher octane than I put in, so I drove to the nearest gas station. I looked behind the cap, and I saw a very small sign that said, "Diesel Only." I let out a string of expletives that would definitely replenish the swear jar.

Back at the McDonalds in this town of less than 7,000 people, I called every car repair shop I could find on Google Maps in a panic. Garage after garage told me they couldn't repair the car that day, even though I explained we had a flight the next day and had a long drive to get to the Sydney airport. A local family sitting next to me came over, and graciously offered to call the garages for me. They called a garage not on Google Maps but whose owner they knew. The owner promptly said he could do the repair if we didn't mind waiting until the end of the day. Incredibly relieved, we repeatedly thanked the family, who even drove ahead of us to the repair shop to make sure we'd make it.

Over the next six hours, the kids and I found and played at every single playground in Cooma. Over, and over, and over, and over again. At the kids' insistence, we returned to that McDonalds two more times – meaning that was their breakfast, lunch, and dinner. Eventually, the car was ready.

We left Cooma with a repaired car around 6 pm and made it to the airport hotel a little after 10:30 pm, exhausted but relieved that we'd make our flight the next morning. It had been a very long day. And now I knew what would happen if one accidentally put regular gas into a diesel.

Australian skiing isn't as good as the Rockies or the Alps. But their resorts were thoroughly modern and fun. Will I go back? Probably next time I'd rather explore Australia's amazing wine country, but I was glad to have visited Thredbo and Perisher.

And our next trip would be to an even more exotic locale than the land down under.

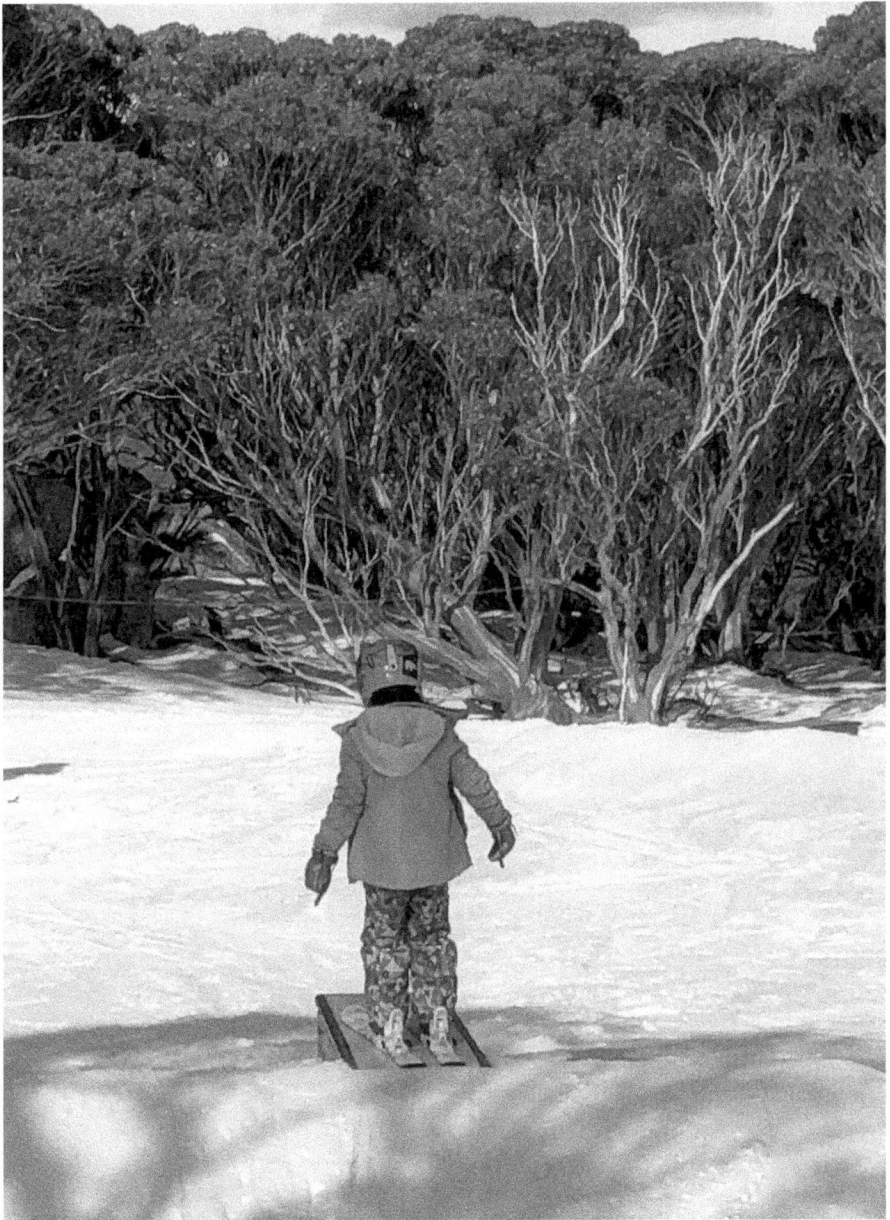

Keira riding a box at Thredbo, Australia

Maddock skiing at Perisher, Australia

Keira before dessert being required to eat Thai food to get dessert

Keira getting dessert after eating Thai food

Chapter 7

Skiing Asia (December 2019)

For my purpose holds to sail beyond the sunset, and the baths of
all the western stars.

Alfred Lord Tennyson

Where to go skiing in Asia? By reputation, Japan is supposed to have the best skiing in Asia. But as our goal was to hit all the continents, I wasn't certain whether or not Japan counts. While it is in Asia, it is also technically a series of islands off the coast. To be safe, I figured I'd should stick to the continent itself. So, that led to the question of where on the continent itself to choose. China is a growing location for skiing, but for whatever reason, travelling to one of the Chinese ski resorts seems more exotic, foreign, and challenging than we were quite ready to do with the kids at that point. And, if China was too much, certainly skiing in Kashmir would be way too much.

Well, what is a more westernized Asian country than China, which has amazing food, and also has ski areas? The answer was obvious to us. South Korea.

Anywhere that has ski areas and makes food as good as Kalbi, Bulgogi, and Bi Bim Bap, must be a cool place to visit. A little quick research showed that there were multiple ski areas relatively close to the capitol of South Korea, Seoul, which makes for easier traveling with the kids. So, we booked a hotel in the Gangnam district in Seoul. (The Gangnam district was made famous by Psy's music video, *Gangnam Style*.) Our trip quickly came together.

We reached out to the hotel before our trip on the details for skiing. Our hotel recommended a tour company that would take the kids and me on a shorter day trip to a local ski area, Jisan Ski Forest, and then a longer day trip to one of the two largest ski areas in South Korea, Yongpyong. This sounded good, and we figured we'd see the sites of Seoul for the rest of the trip.

One concern of ours was the kids, especially Keira, would not want to eat the local food. After the experience of Keira all-but refusing to eat Thai food in Australia, Heather and I were determined to get her used to Korean food. So, we visited the local Korean Restaurant over and over again with the kids. Soon we had a long enough list of Korean foods one or the other kid would like – white rice, Miso soup, Galbi, etc. And, most of all, they loved eating Edamame at the local Korean restaurant in Colorado. Keira (of course) also loved the very expensive Wagyu beef.

As the trip got closer, when we told our friends and our work colleagues we were going to Seoul for Christmas, we kept getting the same question – why? No one questioned us going to Italy for the past Christmas or Australia over the summer. However, everyone kept asking us, why would we go to Seoul? Not ready to tell anyone about the seven-continent chase, we kept our answers vague.

Once we got to Seoul, ironically, everyone in Seoul kept asking us the same question. The hotel staff, puzzled at our presence, asked us why we were visiting South Korea. The tour guides asked us why we were visiting South Korea. No one seemed to believe that an American family, without relatives in South Korea, would ever want to visit South Korea. I'm sure this is the stuff of nightmares for the folks in the South Korean tourism board.

Although South Korea was the opposite of a tourist destination, it was a great place to visit. South Korea is a very friendly country. Almost everyone spoke English at least at a conversational level, and many people were completely fluent. This was true from the maids at the hotel to the rental shop employees at the ski areas. Most signs were in English as well as Korean. South Korea chose English as the second language for a variety of reasons – not least because America had rescued them twice – first from the Japanese at the end of World War 2, and second from the North in the

Korean War. And sitting halfway between a Japanese speaking nation and a Chinese/Mandarin speaking nation it made sense to pick a more neutral second language.

It also helped that the English in South Korea was American English, not British English. When local children would see my Caucasian features, a comparative rarity in Seoul and the nearby ski resorts, they would eagerly approach me excited to practice their English. And their English skills and pronunciation were remarkable. Local children would adorably ask me everything from where I was from to whether I had ever seen the Statute of Liberty.

While I have always been particularly inept at foreign languages, I found myself in an even worse spot in South Korea. The two most important words in any language – "hello" and "thank you" – in Korean are each a combination of five seemingly unrelated syllables. Hello is 안녕하세요 (annyeonghaseyo), pronounced On Yon Ha Say Yo. Thank you is 감사합니다 (gamsahabnida), pronounced Kam Sa Ha Me Da. It wasn't until three quarters of the way through the trip that I had mastered these words to the point where I could start learning other words – such as "yes" and "no." Arabic, as I'd soon learn, was much simpler to my western ears than Korean. Nevertheless, no one seemed to mind my ineptitude at saying hello and thank you, and my inability to say anything else. I felt genuinely welcomed in Seoul and the nearby ski areas.

While the food was great, comically our food training with the kids was all for naught. We were chagrined to never find Edamame anywhere. After all the time conditioning the kids to what we thought was Korean food, we found fewer Korean BBQ restaurants than we thought. It drove us nuts that we never found a place to serve the kids Edamame. But the food was still excellent – and Keira didn't go hungry.

We spent our first two days in the very modern Seoul – a city larger than New York. The second day in Seoul was Christmas Day, and we brought a few small presents for the kids to open. Maddock received a several superhero masks and capes. Much to the delight of the hotel staff and the other hotel guests, Maddock wore superhero capes around the hotel and to every meal while in Seoul.

Among other tourist activities in those first two days, we went to the top of the Lotte Tower (the sixth tallest building in the world that is far higher than the Freedom Tower or the Willis Tower in the United States). Between the towering skyscrapers, electronic billboards, and computer operated toilets – I was expecting ultra-modern ski resorts. Well, I was in for a surprise at our first stop, Jisan Ski Forest.

Having booked the "VIP" tour to Jisan Ski Forest the day after Christmas, we were picked up at the hotel, and driven a half hour north in Seoul by car to an ordinary bus with a decked-out interior, which seemed like it could have been the bus in which they filmed the bus scenes in the *Gangnam Style* music video. (As an aside, unlike Australia where I heard them play "Land Down Under" by Men at Work at several restaurants/bars, I was disappointed that I never heard "Gangnam Style" by Psy while in Gangnam, or frankly anywhere in South Korea.)

After having been shuttled a half hour north, the bus drove two hours south (I could practically see our hotel an hour after we first left it), and eventually arrived at the base of Jisan Ski Forest. It was a small ski area – reminiscent of the ski area I grew up skiing in western New York.

Korean skiing has two things about it that are much better than skiing in the United States. First, the lift attendants at the top of the chairlifts stand by the off-ramp and bow to each chair full of people as they get ready to unload. I can't imagine Colorado lift operators standing by the exit ramp, and politely bowing to each chair as the chair approaches the unload area. Second, the ski areas have compressed air guns at the base of the ski resort, which you can use to blow all the snow off your skis if you want to do so. That's pretty cool, and I'd love to have my skis nice and dry before putting them in my car in the United States.

That said, otherwise skiing was a bit backwards in South Korea. For starters, there was zero natural snow on the ground. The ski runs consisted of 100% man-made snow, with b-netting fencing on both sides of virtually every ski run. This was true not only at the smaller Jisan Ski Forest, but also at the much larger Yongpyong ski resort.

A few days after skiing Jisan Ski Forest, the kids and I went (this time luckily by van with just us) to Yongpyong. Yongpyong had a myriad of hotels at the bottom and had been the host to some of the 2018 Pyeongchang Olympic Events. In spite of steep hills in every direction, the ski runs seemed to be carved into the gentler portions of the hills. While the ski lifts at Jisan Ski Forest seemed oddly old fashion, even if some were technically detachable chairs; the lifts at the much larger Yongpyong Ski Resort were much more modern to American eyes.

However, perhaps the most shocking thing was that neither the rental shop at Jisan nor at Yongpyong had any sense of DIN settings for bindings. As background for those unfamiliar with DIN settings, on one hand, when you take certain types of falls skiing, you want your skis to release from your boots as skis are basically giant torque machines. On the other hand, you don't want your skis to release unintentionally, as that can cause you to fall. Having the right setting on your skis, called DIN settings, optimizes the likelihood of the ski releasing at the right time and not releasing at the wrong time. Proper DIN settings have been carefully studied and tested in the scientific community. In the United States, Europe, and Australia, any rental shop asks you for your weight, your height, and your skiing ability, and then using those inputs adjusts the DIN setting to the universal standards. (Expert skiers often adjust their bindings much tighter, and on the rare cases I'm renting skis, I will always crank up my own DIN setting with the screwdriver on my pocketknife before skiing.)

In the two South Korean rental shops I went to, they basically ignored DIN settings. No one asked any of us for our weight or skiing ability. They basically gave us skis and hoped the DIN setting (if they knew what a DIN setting was) already on the ski was the proper one. I had never heard of such a thing. Fortunately, with my pocketknife I was able to adjust the kids' bindings down and my bindings up to a safer level.

Indeed, the worldwide culture of skiing didn't seem to exist the same way we think of it elsewhere. Everywhere else I had ever skied in the world up to that point, when people asked me where I was from and I responded Colorado, they always asked why I was skiing in their country as they knew how legendary the skiing was in Colorado. No one I spoke with in South Korea had any idea about Colorado or its mountains. Most people had never heard of Colorado or Utah, and didn't think of Alaska as a place to ski. In fact, asking a random ski instructor I met where she thought the best skiing was in the United States, she responded that it must be in Minnesota, because she's heard Minnesota is snowy and cold. In the United States, when skiers think about trips beyond the Rocky Mountains, they daydream about skiing in Alaska, the Alps, or Japan. There seemed to be no equivalent in South Korea. The skiing obsessed ski culture, from what I could tell, seemed less obsessive.

Keira and Maddock remained largely oblivious to most of the backward aspects in my eyes of the skiing here. They loved that they could eat corn dogs, ice cream, and local candies at the lodges at both ski resorts. They were happy enough to ski in this foreign locale. They seemed oblivious to the brief rainfall at Jisan – the first time they had ever been rained on while skiing in the winter. Keira complained a bit about the icy man-made snow – the spoils of learning to ski in Colorado – but my wife and I both told her how lucky she was to practice skiing on tougher snow conditions than anything she'd likely encounter in Colorado. After that, she stopped complaining about the ice.

There were of course other interesting differences. The tour guide made no mention of putting on sunscreen when we were close to Jisan Ski Forest, but returning after skiing Jisan, she told the group not to forget to put moisturizer on our faces. She explained that the sun when skiing causes wrinkles unless you are careful to apply moisturizer afterwards. I will reserve judgment whether the western advice on sunscreen or this eastern advice on moisturizer is better.

I was excited to return to Colorado's snowy and bigger mountains after spending a week in South Korea. Nevertheless, I was such a fan of the compressed air guns, at an American ski industry conference a few weeks later, I told every mountain operations manager I could find about the compressed air guns. I felt like Marco Polo returning from the Orient with tales of civilization and methods of bringing the west up to those levels of civilization. In the years since I've continued to sing the praises of these air guns to numerous ski industry folks, but to this day, my suggestions go unheeded.

I anxiously await Colorado having lift operators who bow to you when you get off the lift, compressed air guns to clean your skis, and spicy pork bulgogi in the base lodge cafeterias. I may, unfortunately, have a while to wait.

Jordan, Keira, and Maddock at YongPyong, South Korea

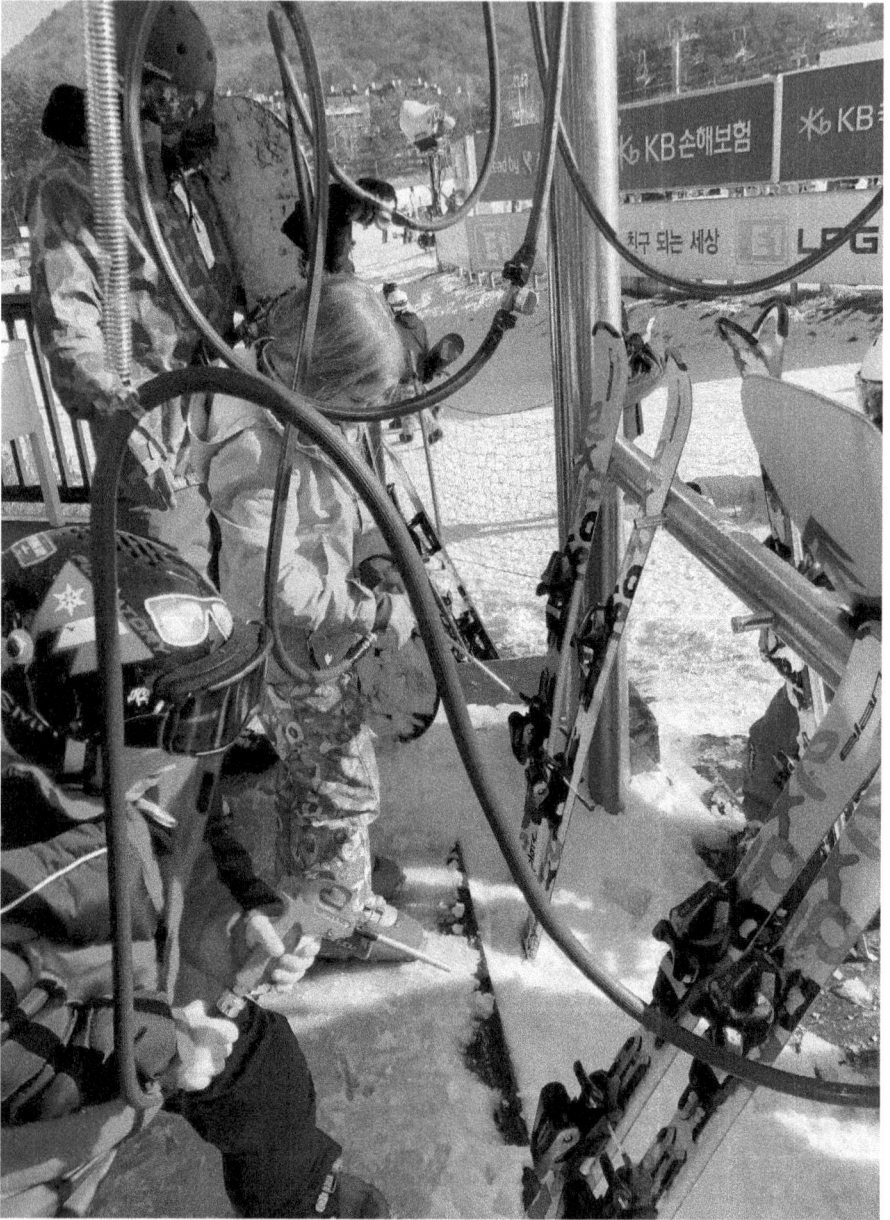

Keira and Maddock cleaning skis at YongPyong, South Korea

Chapter 8

Preparing for Africa (January 2020)

I was convinced of the possibility, but not the inevitability, of success.
Yuichiro Miura

A frica is the second biggest challenge when trying to ski all seven continents. When one thinks of Africa, or at least when I think of Africa, I
think of the great migration on the Serengeti, not of skiing. So, where on
the hottest continent on earth can one ski?

Information is unreliable, but there are probably eight ski areas in Africa.
Africa straddles the equator, so one has to go as far north or as far south
on the continent as possible to ski. There are three tiny ski areas near the
southern end of the continent, with one in Lesotho and two in South Africa.
On the far northern reaches of the continent lie the great Atlas Mountains,
and in the Atlas Mountains there are four ski areas in Morocco and one in
Algeria. Probably. Again, information on skiing in Africa is unreliable.

Based upon my internet research, the biggest ski area in all of Africa was
Oukaimeden, Morocco, with a base elevation of 8,562' and a summit elevation of 10,721'. That sounded pretty impressive. And it was comparatively
accessible. It was only a couple hour drive south from Marrakesh, the fourth
largest city in Morocco. Although there were no direct flights to Marrakesh
from the United States (as far as I could tell), there were multiple direct
flights from Europe.

However, as I dug more into what looked like the "Vail of Africa," it hardly sounded like Vail. Oukaimeden had no grooming and no snowmaking. Its ski lift system consisted of one double chairlift and six surface poma lifts. Reading online reviews of the ski area, I read about donkeys in the parking lot, and how the only toilets at the ski area required a fee to use. It sounded like an interesting place.

Simple flights (with only one connection between Denver and Marrakesh) proved difficult to find. However, we quickly realized that we could fly Denver to Marrakesh via London – as long as we were willing to switch airports in London.

Without snowmaking and with the relatively low base elevation (for the Atlas Mountains) of 8,500', there was no guarantee Oukaimeden Ski Area would be open when we went. So, we knew we might have to try the Africa trip a few times before succeeding. When we coupled the not unlikely possibility of failure on our first try with two other considerations: first, trying to have the kids miss as little school as possible during any year, and second, the fact that Heather was about to start a new job, we decided to book a trip to Morocco last minute, shortly after we got back from South Korea.

With a trip booked just a couple of weeks ahead of time, there was lots do. First off, I knew I should learn something about Morocco. We've all had our embarrassing Google search question moments, but one of my great ones was: "What Language to Do They Speak in Morocco?" I'd seen the movie Casablanca, and everyone spoke English including the German villains. But, setting aside Hollywood, I knew it had been a French colony, so perhaps they spoke French. (Though maybe my knowledge on it being a French colony was also a result of having seen the movie Casablanca on multiple occasions.) Or perhaps they spoke their own language, "Moroccan." Anyone more knowledgeable about the world than me is probably laughing at me at this point, knowing that the answer to my question is "Arabic." This surprised me, considering how far away Morocco was from the Arabian Peninsula. But once I thought about it from the historical perspective of the Arab conquest of North Africa, I suppose it made sense.

With my biggest question, i.e., the language, answered, that led to my second biggest question. As this would be my first time in a majority

Muslim nation, would there be alcohol? As should be obvious by now, I like to drink, but I knew that Islam forbids alcohol. So, right after looking up the language, I looked up the alcohol rules. Online research made Morocco sound like Utah – a place trying to balance a religion that forbade alcohol among its adherents, with its opposite desire to attract tourists who like to drink. From my internet research, it appeared to be a place one could buy alcohol, but with all sorts of rules associated with alcohol purchases and consumption.

Similarly, knowing nothing of the manners and customs of Morocco, I was able to find a (rather lousy) Moroccan travel book on Audible that I quickly absorbed during my commute. I learned some basic and important rules from the book, like tourist women were expected to dress modestly and in long sleeves, and that saying anything bad about the King of Morocco, in public, was a crime.

The next preparation item was to get the kids ready for the food. However, considering that we booked our trip shortly before it would happen, we only had time to take the kids once to a Moroccan Restaurant. We found one in the suburbs of Denver. The kids didn't love the food, but having expanded their palettes from our adventures in South Korea, they seemed game to at least try all the foods. And, as we were only going to be spending half-a-week in Morocco, I figured they could live on humus and pita, if necessary.

There were more preparations in store. If the double chairlift wasn't running, I wanted to make sure the kids were prepared to ride the surface lifts. (Unlike a chairlift that carries a skier in the air back up the mountain, a surface lift pulls a skier on his or her skis/board along the snow back up the mountain.) While many of my friends consider me to be the source of all information related to skiing, I too have to have my friends who I go to with my skiing questions. So, I called my friend who is the professor of ski area operations of Colorado Mountain College. He knows everything about skiing (at least compared to me). I asked him the best place in Colorado to train kids on surface lifts. He recommended Copper Mountain, so we took a day trip to Copper Mountain focused solely on them strengthening their poma lift (technically called a platter lift) and T-Bar lift riding skills.

So, within a few weeks we booked a joint London / Marrakesh trip, made all preparation details, and most importantly, we bought a Lego set of the London skyline for the kids to assemble to learn about London. Unsurprisingly, there's no Lego set for Marrakesh. And then, we were off.

Chapter 9

Skiing Africa (January 2020)

Much have I seen and known.

Alfred Lord Tennyson

The trip began with a fun day in London. It was the kids' first time. We did all the typical tourist activities – eating fish and chips, riding a double decker bus, seeing Trafalgar Square, and taking a boat cruise down the Thames. And I was very relieved to see that although snow conditions had been dire for several weeks near Oukaimeden Ski Area, a snowstorm had just dumped a fresh layer of snow on the Atlas Mountains.

The next morning, getting dressed for the flight, Keira asked why she had to wear long sleeves while I got to wear short sleeves. I told her that it was because she was a girl, and that girls in Morocco couldn't wear short sleeves, but boys could. Indignant, she said: "That isn't fair!" What a great teaching opportunity this presented to me. "Exactly sweetie," I responded. "It isn't fair. That's the point." Of course, I cannot help but wonder if a century from now someone reading this will find some current American practice even less fair. Regardless, my discussion with Keira wouldn't be the last teaching moment of the trip.

We landed in a very nice airport in Marrakesh, and unsurprisingly had the only ski bag in baggage claim. After my experience with ski binding DIN settings in the far more modern South Korea, I was not about to rent ski gear in Africa.

We had a driver hired for the trip, who drove us to a luxury hotel in

Marrakesh. With the exchange rate, nothing in Morocco would be expensive. On the drive, I quizzed the driver on basic Arabic phrases and local customs. He asked me if I knew the name of the King. Thank goodness I literally read the Wikipedia pages on Moroccan history and Moroccan politics that morning while on the flight, so I happily replied Mohammed VI. He was impressed. And, I had learned that as kings go, Mohammed VI was a liberal king – he had a western attitude and was not nearly as oppressive as his father. We had already seen his picture at every turn in the airport, and we continued to see pictures of him in every shop and restaurant.

Morocco is a former French colony, and the French influence was unmistakable. As tourists in the tourist parts of Marrakesh, we were typically greeted in French, not Arabic or English. And what a greeting we would receive in some places. At the hotel, instead of standing in line to check-in, they ushered us to couches and poured green tea for us to consume at our leisure as they checked us in.

Our hotel had three restaurants – an Italian restaurant, a Sushi restaurant, and a Moroccan restaurant. This incidentally got us thinking that this is a fair summary of world cuisine – the three favorite cuisines everywhere in the world seem to be Italian, sushi, and the local cuisine. We knew we would eat well here.

My fears about alcohol were quickly belied in our hotel, which had several fully stocked bars and a happily relaxed attitude towards alcohol. Ordering alcohol was a cinch, and there were lots of excellent local wine. I never expected that Morocco would have a flourishing wine industry.

The attitude towards women, however, shocked me. When the four of us ate dinner, the waiter would ask me what Heather wanted to eat. Heather would respond, and the waiter would only look and talk to me, not Heather. He'd ask me how Heather wanted her meat cooked, she'd respond, he would never look in her direction as he asked me what sides Heather wanted.

When the meal came, I was served first. Then, five-year-old Maddock would be served second. And only after us males had gotten our food; would the waiters then eventually bring out Heather and Keira's dishes. My five-year-old-son was far more important than his mother or older sister.

After the pervasive sexism at restaurant after restaurant, we did have one reprieve. At the sushi restaurant one night, our waiter in surprisingly good English said he had been to Europe, and knows that women get served first in Europe, so he brought out Heather's sushi first. We were so grateful for at least one person who understood chivalry.

The morning after we checked in, we met our driver and headed towards Oukaimeden. After a stop to do the very tourist thing of riding camels, we slowly ascended from the 2,000' elevation plateau on which Marrakesh sat, to the towering and snow-capped Atlas Mountains. As the ski area came into view, it wasn't quite what I expected. In the background, there was a rickety old double chairlift, not looking like it was running, climbing a truly impressive peak. In the foreground there was a large beginner area, all above treeline. There were seven old poma surface lifts going up the beginner pitch in every direction. Only one of them actually appeared to be running. This was not the typical beginner area.

But what was more surprising were the people. The slopes were mobbed with families happily sledding and joyfully throwing snowballs at each other, with hardly a skier in sight. Few things in life make me happier than watching families playing in and enjoying the snow. But where were the skiers?

The sides of the road were even more bizarre. They were littered with people selling ski gear (mostly equipment made in Europe in the 1990s), selling food, selling trinkets, and countless other things. The driver had already had a testy exchange in Arabic with some people about a half mile before the ski area who were blocking the road (we later learned trying to sell ski guide services). But now in the ski area's parking lot, we were accosted by vendors trying to sell us anything and everything imaginable. We ended up having to close the doors of the vehicle so we could put on our ski boots in peace, even if we had very little space.

A pushy man, not in ski boots, in broken English, kept insisting that we hire him as a "guide" for skiing. We kept telling him no, yet he followed us through the parking lot, to the ticket window, and to the base of the one poma lift that was running. I think only when the kids confidently loaded the poma lifts and headed uphill where he couldn't get to us without skis, that he finally left us alone.

We might have been beginners at the social scene, but our driver was not. He instantly bought green tea in a little cup from one of the vendors who swarmed us, and cleverly nursed the little cup for the next couple of hours so at least the tea vendors wouldn't pester him. And it made us feel a little better that the vendors were aggressive with everyone, not just the tourists. On further reflection this made sense, there were few tourists here.

Despite the insanity of the scene, the kids took everything in stride. After all, we had the money, not the kids, so no one pestered the kids to buy anything.

After looking at the rickety old chairlift and the terrain it serviced, Heather told me in no uncertain terms that I was not going to take our children on that lift if it was open. I couldn't say I disagreed.

We bought tickets for about $5 a person to ride the surface lifts, and the kids and I headed out skiing. Although many hundreds of people were on the ski slope, there could not have been more than thirty skiers. And it was instantly apparent, even on the easy terrain serviced by the poma lift, that I was the best skier there. It was just as obvious that Keira (age 7) was the second-best skier on the mountain. A random French lady probably had Maddock beat for third place, but Maddock (age 5) was in a solid fourth place.

On every other turn during every run we hit rocks under the snow. Considering the nearly non-existent snow coverage, we were very relieved that it had recently snowed. Otherwise, skiing would not have been possible. After a few runs, the only running poma lift stopped. It was broken (to be specific for lift nerds like me, there was a bull-wheel de-ropement). Nonplussed, the lift attendant walked over to the poma lift next to it and turned it on. Suddenly, we understood why there were so many poma lifts next to each other.

My son started complaining, not about the people that littered the slope or the countless rocks our skis were hitting, but about the rough ride up the poma lift. So, I offered to pull him by one hand while I held onto the lift with my other hand. This pleased him.

We got in line for the newly turned on poma lift, and we were the second people to ride up the lift. The entire ride I was shouting at families who were hanging out in sneakers standing in the uphill track of the lift to get out of our way, as the lift pulled us straight towards them. Although I didn't know the Arabic term for "get out of the way" or "move" – and it was hardly time for me to rack my brain to try to recall the equivalent French term – my English shouting had the desired effect.

This new lift went a bit higher than the other poma. But the second we got higher on the mountain than the top of the other poma lift, and into fresh powder, the rocks got far worse. Simply, no one had packed down the new snow – and the rocks underneath made the area above all but un-skiable. We unloaded, waited for my daughter on the poma right behind us, and then skied through the rock garden to the point where we were back on the packed down terrain.

I realized at this point that one of the factors to be able to ski all the continents had not previously crossed my mind. In order to put up with skiing on all the continents, one has to get in enough great skiing normally to be willing to endure lousy skiing in some locations. I live in Colorado, and I've skied so much great powder in my life, I'm fine to leave the amaz-ing Rocky Mountains to ski a small snowfield filled with rocks in Morocco. I'm not sure many other people, especially those who do not live in the Rocky Mountains, have sufficiently satiated their appetites for great skiing to be willing to put the time, money, and effort into skiing miserable snow on some of the other continents.

While the snow might have been awful, the people watching in Oukaimeden was fascinating. In Marrakesh, a decent percentage of women (perhaps a quarter) wore no head covering. The majority of women were wearing head scarves (i.e., hijabs), many carefully covering all of their hair as well as their necks. And occasionally in Marrakesh we would see a woman in a burka, with her face entirely concealed. But here in the mountains, far away from the bustling city, burkas were much more common, and there were only two adult women without at least a headscarf. They were Heather and some random French lady who was up skiing (the third best skier on the mountain who I referenced before).

After seven or eight runs, we were done. We were happy to have checked skiing the continent of Africa off our list, and we were ready to return to the more modern Marrakesh. As we headed back to the parking lot, we were again accosted by countless people trying to sell anything and everything imaginable. We were very relieved once our ski boots were off, and we could close the car doors.

Our driver sheepishly asked me as we were driving down about my skis. Someone watching us ski told him that I had the most expensive skis he had ever seen. That person said, our driver unbelievably related, that my skis must have cost 600 Euros. Our driver didn't think that this could possibly be true, but he wanted to know. I responded, honestly, that I had been given the skis for free from a heli ski trip years earlier, but that 600 Euros sounded like a reasonable estimate for the price of the skis. He was amazed.

My wife and I asked the driver if he had ever skied. He said he tried at Oukaimeden once but didn't get it. However, he frequently took his family there to play in the snow. But, although he had been a tour guide / driver for many years, we were the first customers he ever had who asked to go to Oukaimeden. Go figure.

Now that we had skied Morocco, we had an extra day to figure out what to do. With the Sahara Desert on the other side of the Atlas Mountains, and thus not doable as a day trip, our driver suggested that we spend the next day in a desert closer to Marrakesh than the Sahara. So, the next morning the four of us went to a private ranch (with camels and goats) in the middle of the Agafay desert to hike, eat local Berber cuisine, and relax.

There were a handful of other tourists at the desert ranch. There was also a photo shoot going on, with an attractive blonde woman modeling clothes, along with a makeup person, a hair person, and a few photographers for the shoot. It didn't seem to be a surprising spot for a photo shoot, with the stark camel filled desert in the foreground, and the towering snowcapped Atlas Mountains in the background.

But something about the place seemed odd. Curious to see whether the local women were wearing headscarves, burkas, or nothing in the desert, I had been looking around for the local women. I didn't see any. Only local men and the handful of tourists. The next morning, as our guide drove us to the airport, I asked him about where were the women in the desert. He responded to my question with a question. He asked me if I noticed how the houses in that region of the desert didn't have windows. I thought about it for a second, and responded that yes, that sounded right. I didn't think that we had seen windows. Well, he explained, the women were all inside the houses. The houses in the desert didn't have windows, so the women couldn't look out and be tempted by the men who may be visiting the area, he told me. In fact, if we knocked on the door, the women weren't allowed to answer the door, for fear they might come into contact with men not of the house.

A creeping dread fell over me as I slowly processed this information. Here we were, sipping green tea, eating Tajine, enjoying the stunning views, and laughing about the photo shoot with a blonde model – while meanwhile if what our driver said was true, women sat trapped inside the house. A burka seemed extreme enough, but in the desert they apparently took it a drastic step further, literally (if what I had heard was true) locking away their wives and daughters, committing them to a life never knowing what occurred outside the house walls. We were very relieved to be flying back to London. Once back in the United States, although probably only a minute and futile gesture, we donated to a western run girls school in Marrakesh. It wasn't much, but we had to do something to assuage our guilt from paying for a meal in that desert location.[1]

---

[1] It was fascinating to watch what Keira learned from this experience. A month later, I was reading Dr. Hans Rosling's great book, *Factfulness*, which starts with a ten-question quiz about the basics of the world. An example of one of the questions is, by billions of people, how many billions of people live on each continent. These were ten basic questions about the world to which everyone should know the answer. Each question has three choices, and yet in spite of the seeming elementary quality of the questions, people tended to score worse than 33% on the quiz. In other words, people scored worse than a dart throwing monkey. As I knew the premise of the book before I took the quiz, I scored 50%. So, I did better than a monkey, but got a failing grade – a solid F. I gave the quiz to my family, and surprisingly the only one who got a passing grade was Keira. She scored 70%. Trying to understand why my seven-year-old could get a passing grade and I could not, I asked her, for example, how she knew there were a billion less people in Africa than I had guessed. She responded: "Daddy, we've been to Africa. They're mean to women there. So, who would want to live there?" I was about to correct her logic, but then I thought that she got the question right and I got the question wrong, so who was I to judge.

After landing back in London from Marrakesh, we spent another day in London before flying home. We appreciated London all the more now that we were back from the rural regions of Morocco. We rode the London Eye, visited Kings Cross (considering what a Harry Potter fan Keira was at the time), and of course hit many playgrounds.

We completed the second hardest continent. It was time to plan the South America trip and then wrap it up (at least with Keira) with Antarctica in November 2020. We booked a trip to Valle Nevado, Chile for July 2020, and began eyeing an Antarctica trip for November or December 2020. With a little luck, if we could figure out how to get to Antarctica with both kids and skis, we'd soon have this record in a bag. World events, however, would soon conspire against our plans.

Heather, Jordan, Keira, and Maddock at Oukaimeden, Morocco

Jordan and Keira at Oukaimeden, Morocco

PART 3

ANTARCTICA (ROUND ONE)

Chapter 10

An Introduction and Ode to Antarctica (Timeless)

Come my friends, 'T is not too late to seek a new world.
Alfred Lord Tennyson

A ntarctica. The greatest continent on earth.

Before I continue the story of our quest, I must deviate for a chapter in order to extol the virtues of the coolest (both literally and figuratively) place on earth.

The existence of Antarctica had been known for numerous decades before it had ever been seen by human eyes. The Southern Ocean was filled with icebergs, fresh-water ice that can only be born from ice sitting on top of land. So, early explorers knew there must be a large landmass, previously unknown, lurking to the south of all land previously discovered. But no one had actually seen it.

As odd as it may sound today, the first European explorers who mounted expeditions to find this unknown land, brought gifts for the natives on their ships. The plan was to give these gifts to the indigenous population when they arrived. If one puts themselves in the mind set of an explorer in the early nineteenth century, this plan made sense. After all, every place European explorers had discovered on the planet already had native populations. People had made it to such remote locations as Easter Island, New

Zealand, and Hawaii, so it was only natural to assume that Antarctica would already have people living there.

But that's not Antarctica. It's such an inhospitable place, no human eyes had ever glimpsed its shores until the 1820s. To the surprise of the early explorers as they approached Antarctica, there were no natives. Only penguins, seals, and whales.

Like most school children, I had learned a total of one sentence on the politics of Antarctica in grade school. I learned only that it was a demilitarized continent that no country owns. So, it was a surprise to me when Heather and I first made it down to Antarctica in 2010 to learn about the great political jockeying over the continent.

The political jockeying is easiest to describe using the Antarctic Peninsula as an example. The Antarctic Peninsula is the most visited part of the continent. The peninsula is much like a mountainous Florida. It is a large peninsula that juts out into the warmest waters of the area and has the warmest climate. It's also only a two-day boat-ride or a few hours plane flight from the southern tip of South America. It is far closer to Argentina and Chile than any other part of Antarctica is to its other neighbors of South Africa, Australia, and New Zealand.

Its comparative proximity and warmth makes the peninsula one of the more coveted spots in Antarctica. As such, the Antarctic Peninsula is claimed by no fewer than three different countries – Argentina, Chile, and Great Britain. And indeed, just as in the corner of American maps is a box with Alaska, in the corner of Chilean maps is a box with Chile's claimed portion of Antarctica. The portion Chile claims as its own looks like a pizza slice – it follows the lines of longitude from the shores of Antarctica ending in a triangular point at the South Pole. Maps in Argentina are similar with its pizza slice of territory (overlapping the Chilean pizza slice) in the corner of its maps. Great Britain's claim also looks like a pizza slice – starting wide at the coast and narrowing along exact lines of longitude to the South Pole. And, as you've probably already guessed where this is going – Argentina, Chile, and Great Britain all claim overlapping pizza slices of the same territory.

Other countries have claimed their own pizza shaped slices of other parts of Antarctica too. All territorial claims of all countries thus converge on one spot – the center of the pizza pie, so to speak – the South Pole. And this leads to the typically brilliant F-you approach of the United States. Faced with numerous competing claims for Antarctica without one of its own, the United States built a large station on the South Pole itself. This station sits atop all other countries' claims to Antarctica. Its very presence cries out the message – the United States does not recognize any other countries' claim on Antarctica. Implicitly although not explicitly, America's South Pole base declares the entire continent to be an American continent.

The competing territorial claims of Antarctica lead to some interesting results for visiting tourists. How does a country establish territoriality? One key method is by stamping passports. The Falkland Islands war, after all, began over a dispute on stamping passports. So, various countries with Antarctica bases virtually beg the tourist ships to stop by their research bases so they can stamp the tourists' passports. From our 2010 Antarctica trip, my old passport book has stamps of countries from Argentina to Russia, to which I had never actually been.

But these passport stamps are optional, and going to Antarctica means literally going off the grid. You go through customs in the airport departing for Antarctica, but when you arrive, there's no airport. There's no customs. No border control. You are, in reality, in no country. There is just ice. There are no laws, no governments, no police. It's just you, the penguins, and the ice.

Why all this political jockeying for Antarctica? The answer is simple. It's all about future resources. Today, the extreme cold and miles of ice make it virtually impossible to profitably extract resources. But with fifty or one-hundred more years of technological advances, coupled with climate change, it's certainly quite possible that Antarctica's abundant natural resources, for better or worse, could be profitably extracted. Thus, countries are slowly preparing their territorial claims for the day in the future when Antarctica could be profitable.

There are two views of the politics of Antarctica, and I certainly take (and describe above) the more cynical view. Taking the less cynical view for two sentences, in 1959, the Antarctica Treaty was signed providing that no country would make further claims to the continent. The treaty has reduced the political jockeying over the continent and helps protect it.

However, the treaty does not require signatory countries to renounce their claims. More importantly, if the long history of international politics has taught us anything, it is that many if not most treaties only last as long as the economics or demographics underlying them remain relatively constant. Perhaps the greatest and most successful international agreement of all times – the Congress of Vienna – only lasted 99 years. At that rate, the Antarctica treaty has less than three decades of life left in it. It's a wonderful treaty and the signatory governments should stick to it, but like any international treaty, it is fragile.

In any event, as fascinating as the politics of Antarctica are, the wildlife is even more crazy. I was first drawn to the idea of visiting Antarctica from a wildlife story I heard from a friend at a party. Between the passage of time since I heard the story many years ago, and the fact that I'm sure both my friend and I were drunk when she related the story, take this story with a grain of salt. Nevertheless, hopefully the story encapsulates one of the great reasons why people are so fascinated by this forbidding land.

She told me that while on her Antarctica trip, she was on a wind-swept rocky beach with the other members of her tour group. There were penguins waddling around, and seals belly flopping to and thro. Suddenly, from across the bay, a giant serac (an ice chuck the size of a 40-floor building) calved off the glacier. It crashed into the icy waters. Her guides started yelling to the people, "run uphill!" As they started to run uphill away from the shore, it was a mad scramble of penguins, seals, and people. All three animals seemed to have the same goal and to be assisting each other in escaping the giant wave approaching the shore. As the large wave emanating from the falling serac crashed harmlessly on the beach below them, the three groups of now intermingled animals breathed a collective sigh of relief. Then, realizing the danger was over, the penguins, people, and seals each separated themselves from the other species, and went back to minding own their business. For one short moment, she had been just another animal, working in tandem with the native animals, to survive in this harsh land.

Heather and I had no adventure of equal magnitude to that story when we visited in 2010, which was probably a good thing. However, having never spent any time around penguins, on that trip we discovered they were the most extraordinary creatures. Penguins in Antarctica have no land-based predators. So, on land, they have no fear. One could walk right up to them, and they do not care at all. While in the ocean they are at risk of being the food of leopard seals. However, without having any predators on land, they see themselves as invincible once out of the water and on the snow-covered ground.

It is hardly an understatement to say that penguins are one of the most beloved animals on earth. They star in countless postcards, comics, and Christmas ornaments. Until you've spent a lot of time around these cute little creatures to realize how truly smelly they are, their appeal seems utterly irresistible. And even with their stench when you're close to them, they're still pretty hard not to love.

Why are penguins so beloved? They're just birds, after all. Seals are mammals – much closer relatives to us than penguins – yet we hardly hold seals in the same esteem as penguins.

Contrary to the suggestions of the wonderful documentary March of the Penguins, I don't think the appeal of penguins is due to their seasonal monogamy, mutual parenting, or tender care for their young. That is true of many species, none of which people adore as much as penguins. Rather, I think the primary appeal of penguins comes from a more simple and primeval association.

Penguins are the only animal that walk like us.

Sure, they walk like a drunk version of us, but their gait is like our gait. Other two-legged creatures – think of an ostrich – move nothing like a person. But penguins resemble us. Penguins look almost like short people, and they move like us. Adorably, their wings separate to the sides to help them balance as they walk – something every toddler (and drunk) does as well to assist with the unnatural upright gait we share with penguins. We identify with penguins because they walk like us.

This makes it shocking to see a penguin swimming. While they waddle/walk like a cute miniature version of us, in the water they are an entirely different creature. They are fast and agile. Their wings spread out, and they appear to fly through the water like most birds fly through the air. They covert from a semi-comical creature on land to a majestic creature in the oceans.

Their tuxedo appearance – white bellies and chests, with black backs and legs – probably further adds to their appeal. This coloration, however, is no accident. It wasn't meant to mimic human clothing norms. Rather, it's pure Darwinian evolution. A penguin's camouflage is for where it is needs camouflage – in the ocean. When close to the surface in the ocean, looking down into the depths of the water, the depths look only black. And being deeper in the water staring up at the surface, the surface looks bright. So, a swimming penguin from above tends to blend in with the vast depths of the ocean, and from below tends to blend in with the bright sky. Their tuxedo appearance is just camouflage to protect them from detection by the hungry leopard seals, and aid the penguins in their hunt for smaller prey.

As much as I love talking about penguins, this chapter has still yet to address, what in my mind, is the greatest part of Antarctica. It's not its history and politics. Nor is it the animal population. Rather, it is the majestic scenery, that is downright alien in appearance compared to most of the earth.

Living in Colorado and having climbed extensively in the Pacific Northwest prior to my first Antarctica trip, I was quite familiar with glaciers – permanent and slowly moving collections of snow. Colorado has many tiny glaciers. The volcanoes of the Pacific Northwest have much larger glaciers spotted with crevasses. The biggest of these crevasses, fissures in the snow, are large enough to swallow a decent sized skyscraper. These crevasses have a brilliant emanating emerald color, nearly impossible to reproduce in photographs or videos. They are a sight to behold.

Before I went to Antarctica, I thought I knew snow and ice. I was wrong. The glacial monstrosities I knew well from America are only the tiny outlets of the far bigger ice sheets that cover most of the Antarctic continent. Ice sheets primarily exist in Antarctica and Greenland, and most of the fresh water in the world is stored in these land covering behemoths. The glaciers I knew from the United States paled in scale to the endless ice sheets of Antarctica. The first time I went to Antarctica, I felt like a person who had only seen small lakes staring for the first time at the ocean. The size of the ice sheets, like the size of the ocean, is practically incomprehensible.

But Antarctica is so much more than land-eating ice sheets. With the perennial cold, the snow never melts. So, in the space of a few hundred feet between mountainous cliffs and the ocean, a pure white glacier teaming with emerald-colored crevasses forms.

As Heather describes the scenery in Antarctica, it is unlike anywhere. For most other locations on earth, one marvels at the skill of the great photographers in capturing the beauty of a landscape that is not readily apparent when one looks at that landscape, no matter how pretty that landscape might already be. A great photographer, after years experimenting with the perfect lens for each spot, spends days capturing the perfect split-second image of the location. No matter how many times I've gazed at the various famous arches near Moab, they've never had the lighting captured in the Peter Lik photographs of them. But Antarctica, to the naked eye, is always the perfect image. There is no need for great photographers in Antarctica. It always looks to the naked eye like the perfect photograph.

It is probably futile for me to try to put into my own words the magnificence of the scenery, but please allow me to do my best to attempt to describe it in a portrayal of one location in our first visit. My favorite spot was colloquially referred to as the iceberg graveyard. The geography and ocean currents by this shallow cove resulted in currents and wind bringing floating icebergs into its grasp. Once in its grasp, the comparatively shallow sea bottom captured the icebergs. The icebergs would get stuck in the cove. Once captured, the icebergs would subsequently spend the next century or two slowly melting until they dislodged or melted out.

We took zodiac boats (10–14-person rigid inflatable rubber motorboats) to zoom around and under these slowly melting icebergs that filled the iceberg graveyard. The only way I can think to describe this bizarrely fantastic experience is by analogy. We were like ants in a mushroom patch. The mushrooms were these exquisite emerald blue icebergs surrounding and towering over us. And we were mere ants in comparison to them. It was extraordinary.

From the extreme environment to the penguins, from the icebergs to the ice sheets, this was the most extraordinary place upon which I had ever placed my eyes. After my first visit, I could not wait to return again.

Chinstrap penguin parent and chick in Antarctica

The Antarctica Peninsula

Chapter 11

Logistics and the Pandemic Pause (February 2020 to December 2021)

How dull it is to pause … to rust unburnished, not to shine in use.
As tho' to breathe were life.

Alfred Lord Tennyson

The logistics for skiing six of the seven continents are comparatively simple. Aside from luck, even Africa is not too tough to pull off. The logistics of skiing Antarctica, on the other hand, are a whole different story. If you look at a globe from the bottom, you will see that there are five countries that sit across the Southern Ocean from Antarctica. Chile and Argentina lie to the north of the Antarctic Peninsula and are the nearest countries to Antarctica. The other three countries directly to the north of Antarctica – Australia, New Zealand, and South Africa, each are more distant from the shores of Antarctica, but each are used to access their respective sides of the Antarctic continent.

While people access Antarctica via all five countries, owing to the proximity of Argentina and Chile, the vast majority of tourists depart from South America. Occasional planes from Punta Arenas, Chile, fly across the Southern Ocean to King George Island, just north of the Antarctic Peninsula. From there, an overnight boat ride brings one to Antarctica.

To keep using my mountainous Florida analogy from the prior chapter, flying into King George Island is the equivalent of flying into Key West, and then taking an overnight boat ride to the continent of North America at the mainland of Florida. This is how Heather and I accessed Antarctica in 2010.

More common, ships leave Ushuaia, Argentina, the world's southernmost city, and make the arduous two-day journey across the Drake Passage. The Drake Passage is probably the world's worst ocean crossing, as the warm waters of the Pacific and Atlantic Ocean fight it out with each other, and with the cold waters of the Southern Ocean. This creates gigantic swells that knock even the sturdiest boats to and thro. However, owing to the lesser costs, coupled with the fact that flights are frequently delayed into and out of King George Island, this awful boat journey is the more popular way to access the Antarctica Peninsula than flying from Punta Arenas. It's also typically much less expensive.

As we had been to the Antarctic Peninsula, as well as the facts that it has the most pleasant weather in Antarctica, has giant mountains, and has the vast majority of Antarctic tourism, we focused on trying to find a boat (or plane) from South America. Skiing the Antarctic Peninsula seemed like the logical location to check off skiing the greatest continent on earth.

It is hard to tell, but there are probably somewhere between fifty to seventy tourist ships that operate in Antarctica in any given season. In addition, there are a few land based operations that welcome tourists. Surely one of them would agree to let the kids and me ski.

Both Heather and I spoke with seemingly countless ski and climbing guides, ship operators, and travel agents. Very few of them permitted skiing. And very few of them permitted young children. Trying to find one that did both seemed downright impossible.

Email after email, and call after call, we were not having any luck. In one comical exchange, speaking to a travel agent who claimed to specialize in custom Antarctica tours, after we explained our goal, she responded: "that's a bit of an unusual request." Exacerbated, I sighed and tried to politely explain that "we're going for a world record, so it has to be more unusual than just a bit unusual. It's a unique request – that's the whole point of a world record!" She, unsurprisingly, came up empty with solutions.

After seemingly endless calls and emails, a ski guide named Jorge Kozulj from Bariloche, Argentina, who we contacted, said he thought this would be feasible. He worked with an operator, Ice Axe Expeditions, that rented out a large portion of the first boat in November headed to Antarctica for die-hard skiers such as myself. After some begging and cajoling from both Jorge and me, Ice Axe Expeditions agreed to take Keira. They would not take Maddock as he was too young. So, at least for Keira, we had a shot.

We booked a trip for Keira and me departing November 2020 through Ice Axe Expeditions.[2] We agreed all four of us would repeat the trip as soon as Maddock was old enough to be allowed to join. We likewise had booked a trip to Valle Nevado, Chile, for the summer of 2020. Everything was now lined up for Keira to check off continent six in July 2020 and continent seven in November 2020. Within nine months, we would have the world record completed.

★ ★ ★

---

[2] As an aside, I found buying travel insurance for this trip rather interesting. How dangerous is a trip like this in the mind of math geeks? Well, let's see what the underwriters at the travel insurance company think. If you go to Antarctica, serious travel insurance is a must as the cost of an emergency evacuation from a continent of ice without a single real hospital is astronomical. Of course, travel insurance covers cancelled trips, lost baggage, and a host of non-evacuation items, but no one steps foot on Antarctica without making sure they have travel insurance covering emergency evacuation.

The skiing part of the trip, at least according to the travel insurance amounts, couldn't be too dangerous. The cost of the required travel insurance for the two of us without skiing (prior to COVID-19) was $1,829, while the skiing added a mere $22 to the cost of the travel insurance. And ironically, of the $1,829, it placed my premium at $1,109 while Keira's was a mere $720. According to the underwriters, Antarctica was more dangerous for me than for Keira. And skiing it only amounted to a $22 risk for both of us.

Then the COVID-19 pandemic happened.

Most readers will need no introduction to the COVID-19 pandemic. However, on the off-chance this book is beloved by some a century from now, I figured I should devote a paragraph to describing the COVID-19 pandemic and its impact, as a reader in the 2100s may be as unfamiliar with the pandemic as I am about the Dust Bowl. After all, I know the Dust Bowl occurred and impacted countless lives, but I know hardly anything about it. So here goes, the COVID-19 pandemic in one paragraph.

In March 2020, an influenza-like-illness virus, technically named SARS-CoV-2, began to sweep through the world. There were two opposing views of the pandemic. One view is that the virus, rivaled only by the Spanish Flu of 1918, created the worst pandemic since medicine became a science. The virus killed many hundreds of thousands of people in America alone, and many millions of people throughout the world. It was a tragedy of unfathomable proportions. The other view is that governments ignored a century of epidemiological science, and in a fit of fear and hubris imposed endless irrational restrictions in a futile attempt to stop an unstoppable virus and control the populace. For just one of countless examples, Colorado politicians decided that in-person schooling was "not essential," so Keira, Maddock, and their classmates were denied an education for many months, while liquor stores were deemed by the same politicians to be "essential," so adults could continue to buy alcohol in-person inside liquor stores.

Like many stories with two opposing narratives, both versions were tragically accurate. But enough on the depressing topic of COVID-19. It's time to get back to the story of how it impacted our quest.

At the start of the pandemic, most people (including us) were sure that the pandemic would last only a few weeks. It was unfathomable that this brief event would interfere with our summer plans. The weeks, however, quickly dragged into months. Chilean travel restrictions and ski area closures stopped the summer 2020 Valle Nevado trip. Not to fear, we thought. Keira and I could ski permanent snowfields in the South American summer on our way down to Antarctica in November 2020. However, in spite of incredible efforts by Ice Axe Expeditions, the November Antarctica trip was likewise cancelled by Argentinian travel restrictions.

While disappointed, we had built in over a year buffer in our record quest. We rebooked the Antarctica trip for November 2021, with every confidence it would move forward. We planned to have Keira ski with me in the mountains above Ushuaia to check off South America before boarding the ship for Antarctica and completing the quest. Keira spent the Colorado summer getting ready. She was interested in skiing a 14,000' peak in Colorado. With me carrying up her and my skis and ski boots, she climbed, summitted, and then skied down the 14,271' tall Quandary Peak just south of Breckenridge. One of the major online ski publications, SnowBrains, had a wonderful article on her accomplishment.

Similarly, I started working with Keira on basic snow travel and crevasse rescue skills. Keira was an accomplished skier at this point, but Antarctica presents as many mountaineering challenges as skiing challenges. In order to backcountry ski in Colorado in the summer, Keira was already becoming comfortable with using an ice axe while ascending, the key purpose of which is to stop any serious fall. But in Antarctica, Keira should have a basic understanding of dealing with crevasses. If either I or a guide fell in a crevasse, I wasn't expecting her to pull us out. Similarly, I wasn't expecting that if she fell in a crevasse that she would know how to ascend the rope to rescue herself. But, if any of these contingencies occurred, I wanted her to be at least familiar with the concepts. I wanted her to be at worst neutral, at best an asset, in an emergency crevasse rescue – not a liability.

So, we started casual rock climbing so she'd start to have a basic comfort with a harness, carabiners, rappelling, and working with a rope. More important, we went to cornices in July, Colorado's best proxy for large crevasses, to review basic crevasse rescue skills. We went through how to prussik hitch climb out of a crevasse (that is, how to use two smaller ropes on the main climbing rope to ascend the rope out of a crevasse). I taught her how to build a snow anchor. And I taught her how to build up the pulley systems to pull someone out of a crevasse.

Our training was going well, and we were both beyond excited for our upcoming trip. However, for a second year in a row owing to the seemingly endless government imposed COVID-19 restrictions, the Argentinian government again did not permit tourist ships to go through Ushuaia. Our 2021 plans were thwarted. The trip was off.

Twice Keira and I thought we were going to pull off the trip, and twice our plans were crushed. There was some crying in our house when the November 2021 trip was cancelled. In order to break the world record, Keira had to ski all seven continents by summer 2022, and this was no longer possible.

At that point, I more-or-less threw in the towel. Keira would not break the world record. We had tried. And in spite of our best efforts, we had failed.

In late November 2021, the first landing of a large commercial plane, an Airbus A340, in Antarctica made international news. A work colleague of Heather's sent her an article on it and the adventure company who pulled it off – White Desert. White Desert was founded by an Antarctic adventurer who held several world records, and although technically a British company, ran its operation out of Cape Town, South Africa. So, Heather started researching a different option than what we had previously focused – accessing Antarctica not via boat or plane from South America, but rather via plane from South Africa. This was a very different way to see Antarctica. Instead of seeing Antarctica's coast, if it worked, this trip would bring Keira and me to the interior of the continent.

After some back-and-forth, White Desert agreed that Keira and I could join them and bring our skis. Maddock was too young, so this would be a daddy-daughter trip. So, for a third time Keira and I booked a trip, for January 2022, to head down to Antarctica.

This gave us only a short window to train. Not wanting to have to pull my regular weight out of a crevasse or God forbid have to carry Keira a long distance, I knew I had to get down to fighting weight. In the month we had to prepare, I was able to drop two belt notches – not as good as I could have done with more time but a lot better than nothing.

Similarly, I needed to get Keira ready in a hurry. I tried to ski as much with Keira as possible – both in-bounds and backcountry. We dropped a rope off our back porch, so Keira could practice rappelling down and prussik hitch climbing up – both key skills for heading into glaciated terrain. We spent more time with ice axes, practicing self-arrests, and reviewed roped travel techniques. Little did I know that this would all be largely unnecessary, but our practices did lead to a hysterical exchange. On Caribou Hill in Colorado, practicing in the snow and wind, I asked Keira – "what happens if the guide falls into a crevasse." She responded, "then I die." "No," I yelled, "that's a horrible answer! You don't die. That's why we're training!" She looked at me and laughed – "Dad, I said 'dive,' not 'die,'" she explained through the wind. Relieved, I agreed with her – yes, you "dive down in self-arrest position, you don't 'die.'" I blamed her enunciation, she blamed my hearing, and we both blamed the wind for the miscommunication.

Here we were. After waiting nearly two years to get our next continent in, we were about to be back in the race.

Keira skiing her first 14er, Mount Quandary, Colorado

Chapter 12

Cape Town (January 2022)

I am a part of all that I have met.

Alfred Lord Tennyson

K eira and I flew from Denver to Newark and then from Newark to Cape Town. Heather and I had flown into Cape Town many years earlier in order to spend a week wine tasting in South Africa's amazing wine regions near Cape Town, as well as spending three days in northeast South Africa on safari. So, while I had never stayed in Cape Town itself, I had a vague sense of it, and of South Africa more generally. While the purpose of the trip was Antarctica, I knew there would be some real time in South Africa before and afterwards.

In the craziness of the COVID-19 time, regardless of whether we felt sick or not, we were required to get a test for COVID-19 and present it at customs to get into South Africa and to get back into the United States. Happily, we both tested negative. With a plethora of paperwork in hand, as is required for travel with one parent and child, getting into South Africa was a breeze.

We were scheduled to go down to Antarctica for 7 days and had given ourselves a few days cushion in Cape Town on either end. That cushion time is critical. White Desert asked us to make sure we had that cushion time, and after Heather and my last trip to Antarctica, we knew doing so would be the wise choice. Travelling to Antarctica, after all, is not like travelling anywhere else in the world.

There are no airports in Antarctica. Thus, the standard instrumented landing done by all commercial airlines at all commercial airports worldwide is not possible. Rather, all landings and takeoffs must be done not by instruments but by sight, what pilots refer to as VFR. As such, one needs a weather window of good visibility long enough to justify the flight (and jet fuel) from the embarkation point to Antarctica and back. When Heather and I flew down to Antarctica from Punta Arenas, Chile, back in 2010, Heather and my flight left on time. But owing to low level clouds, we ended up spending an extra 2 ½ days in Antarctica because the flight couldn't come back in to pick us up for that time. We hardly complained about getting an extra 2 ½ days in Antarctica, but it did throw our travel back to the United States into total disarray. If one is planning to fly to Antarctica, patience and a flexible schedule are essential.

As such, we knew we would be spending a good bit of time in South Africa before and after our trip. With the COVID-19 pandemic continuing and its corresponding impacts on poverty and crime, the U.S. State Department had issued its highest warning for travel to South Africa – deeming the country unsafe due to crime and violence. Heather, concerned by this warning, insisted that Keira and I stay at the fanciest large hotel in Cape Town, on the logical reasoning that a top-of-the-line hotel would have top of the line security. I asked White Desert for their recommendations, and they recommended the One & Only Cape Town. So, unlike the Holiday Inn Express and Best Western style hotels that I normally book, we booked ourselves at the Dubai-based luxury hotel chain One & Only, which incidentally had Africa's only Nobu Restaurant.

We arrived in Cape Town to an email that our Antarctica trip days had already been rescheduled due to weather, so we would be spending more time in Cape Town before heading down, and less time on the way out. Knowing Antarctica, this hardly surprised me.

After clearing customs, picking up our duffel bags of Antarctic clothing and the only ski bag in the entire South African airport, we went to the hotel. The district in which our hotel was located, the V&A Waterfront, was a thriving and bustling hub of affluence and luxury. While there was a strong private security presence both at the hotel and throughout the V&A

Waterfront district – this hardly seemed necessary. It was an area of yachts, fancy shopping malls, great sushi, and lots of seals happily swimming in the ocean or lounging on the docks. Our hotel was located right on the salt-water canal off the ocean, and Keira and I rented stand-up paddle boards to paddle the full length of the canal. The biggest threat in the canal were the otters, who apparently had a mean streak. The biggest problem with any aggressive otters is that one wasn't allowed to hit them with the paddles as they are apparently endangered. Although we saw several otters, they fortunately did not bother us as we paddleboarded by them.

As we were headed to the interior of Antarctica, not to an area near the ocean, we would not see penguins while in Antarctica. Penguins, after all, are sea going creatures. They feed in the food rich oceans, but mate and raise their young in the safety provided by land in close proximity to the water. By analogy, the land was their home location, and the ocean was their work location – with a commute done at a slow walking pace over snow.

Since everyone's first question when you go to Antarctica is about the penguins, I thought it was crucial that Keira be able to see penguins, even if not in Antarctica. Fortunately, African Penguins are plentiful near Cape Town, so Keira could tell her friends all about penguins, even if it wasn't Antarctica Penguins. So, we arranged a tour to see the African Penguins. We had a fun tour to the north side of Boulders Beach – with Keira's highlight being the ability to see countless African Penguins, and my highlight being able to talk with the tour guide about South African history and politics. He grew up under Apartheid, he was labeled as "colored" by the regime and had a wealth of fascinating firsthand experiences to relate from the Apartheid era and the post-Apartheid era.

Incidentally, at the start of the pandemic, Heather and I got a live-in au pair from overseas. (Without a live in au pair during the school closures, Heather and I would not have both been able to maintain our jobs. And we quickly got used to having an au pair.) Our current au pair was from South Africa, and her parents lived in Cape Town. We were excited to meet her parents, and they were excited to meet Keira and me. So, the day after the penguin tour, a regular pick-up truck (what South Africans call a 'bak-kie') drove up to the One & Only for us to meet our au pair's parents. In the hotel's parking area filled with Mercedes and BMWs, the pick-up truck happily stood out like a sore thumb. We met our au pair's parents, and they took us to the south end of the same Boulders Beach.

Instantly, Boulders Beach became my favorite beach in the world. The beach was covered with Flintstone size boulders. Maneuvering around the boulders was tricky but doable. But the amazing part was that there were hundreds of penguins, interspersed with the people. As penguins have incredibly sharp beaks for hunting, giving them twelve inches of space is prudent. But they happily walked right next to people, and people happily walked right next them. It was a surreal experience.

Keira, who is practically a fish, loved swimming, while I watched the penguins. Keira said that the beach would have been even better if I had gotten into the water with her.

This description so far of the location unfairly leaves out the physical beauty of the Western Cape of South Africa. It resembles Hawaii, with rugged beautiful green mountains falling steeply into the deep blue ocean waters. And beyond the beautiful scenery, there are countless amazing animals at every turn. In addition to the seals, penguins, and otters already mentioned, we saw countless baboons and dolphins. Keira couldn't resist after watching the baboons, she repeatedly would jump on my back for a ride like a baboon baby.

I was also pleased that after Keira's reaction to the overwhelming sexism we experience in our Morocco trip, this visit to Africa would show her that our Moroccan experience was not indicative of the whole continent. While South Africa has its numerous societal struggles, it was great for Keira to see that women were treated as well here as the other places around the globe we had visited. Keira would no longer unfairly classify the entire of continent of Africa as sexist based upon our observations of one very limited region of Morocco.

After several days of enjoying the tourist life in South Africa (and doing lots of homework with Keira to make up for the missed school), our Antarctica trip was finally about to begin. As had sadly become standard, we were required to yet again take another COVID-19 test to travel to Antarctica. While for all travel a positive test result was always a concern, it didn't strike me anymore as much of a concern. Neither Keira nor I felt the least bit sick. While we were both vaccinated for COVID-19 (and required to be vaccinated to go on the trip), this didn't provide much comfort as the vast majority of people I knew who had gotten COVID-19 had gotten it after they had been vaccinated. That said, we weren't sick in the least, so what was there to worry about? Likewise, being young and healthy, we had zero concern about catching COVID-19 for its health consequences on us – rather our only concern was that having COVID-19 could prevent us from travelling.

Keira at Boulders Beach, South Africa

Chapter 13

Quarantined (January 2022)

Challenge is what makes man, and there can be no challenge without the risk of failure.

Yuichiro Miura

As arranged by the tour operator, a friendly nurse came to our hotel room the morning before we were to depart for Antarctica to administer our COVID-19 tests. She took nasal swabs, and we all waited for the results that took 15 minutes, happily chatting with the nurse about our travel plans and her interest in seeing the United States. 10 minutes after our nasal swabs, she smiled and told us everything was looking good. And then, a minute later, she called me over and showed me that there was a faint line on the test showing that Keira had tested positive.

Keira burst out crying – not for any fear of COVID-19 as neither of us had any – but at the prospect that Antarctica would be cancelled. A positive test result would mean that we wouldn't be allowed to board the plane. We rushed down to the concierge, with Keira in tears and me close to tears as well, to see if he could arrange a rush series of COVID-19 tests to try to show that Keira's first test was a false positive. He had a new nurse on the road almost instantly to come to our hotel room to retest Keira. I emailed White Desert in a panic. And right before the nurse the concierge arranged to do the second round of testing, I got a call from White Desert. We could not go to Antarctica, they reported. Their consulting physicians had a very strict rule that if someone tested positive to any COVID-19 test, we could not travel.

I knew I had to tell Keira. I looked at her, and I told her Antarctica would not happen, and she would not break the world record. While she had been sad the last two times the trips were cancelled, both times were months before the trip. Here we were, half-way across the world and a day away from getting down to Antarctica, and now we could not go.

Keira began to sob. Through tears she pleaded with me. "Daddy, what if I promise to stay ten feet away from everyone else?" "Daddy, please let them have me go, I promise to wear a mask every second of the trip." But I knew as painful as it was, our chance was over, and I couldn't avoid using the "d" word. "It's done Keira," I explained. The trip and the record would not happen. She cried and cried into the hotel pillow.

The concierge and the nurse for the new round of tests arrived at our hotel room. I figured we should retest regardless, but the same results came back – Keira was positive and I was negative. Seeing our distress, the concierge looked at me, and told me that he was a father of several girls, and he knew what we were going through. And he told me that while he spent his weekdays as the concierge at the hotel, on the weekends he served as a minister. He said that if he could help in any way, he would. With Heather a continent away and fast asleep as it was 2 am in Colorado, having the concierge, an adult, to speak with was a godsend.

The loss of Antarctica was the biggest blow, but we soon learned of the second blow. Although Keira was not sick in the slightest, South African regulations required the two of us to quarantine. So, we literally went from about to fly down to Antarctica after sight-seeing throughout the Western Cape to being stuck in our hotel room. Although the entire staff was kind, we unavoidably felt like Pariahs – with the staff ordered to keep a distance from us as they brought us meals – with us not allowed to enter the hall and them not allowed to enter the room.

While Keira cried out her disappointment in the few hours after the positive test result and I remained comparatively stoical, she seemed to take the disappointment better than me over the next days. Stressed by being locked up, by having to act strong in front of my daughter, being starved of adult interaction, and most importantly, devastated that in spite of all our efforts Antarctica had just alluded our grasp – I struggled to not let my negative emotions overwhelm me.

There we were, stuck in Africa.

The balcony of our hotel room provided light early in the morning, so Keira and I made sure to get as much Vitamin D as we could before the sun moved behind the hotel wall placing the balcony in shade. I exercised as much as I could in the hotel room, with the ski bag turning into a makeshift barbell, and Keira hopping on my back as I did squats for additional weight. We worked on homework, played endless games of cards, and I let Keira watch more television than would have been appropriate in any other circumstance. The hotel delivered a backpack full of kids' toys, which helped keep Keira entertained. We reread the same books over and over.

While I usually try to work as little as possible on vacation, I found the best parts of my days were work calls. I was so excited to deal with stressful client calls, difficult attorneys on the other side of my cases, and strategy sessions where there were no right answers. Doing the stressful portions of my job seemed much more pleasant than being locked up in the hotel room with nothing to do, and little to think about other than the overwhelming disappointment.

After a few days in the hotel room, without any housekeeping and with endless meals in the room, I asked the housekeeping department for a vacuum cleaner. They left one for me in the hallway, and I took it into our now messy hotel room and vacuumed. There I was, in one of the fanciest resorts in all of sub-Saharan Africa, and I was vacuuming the hotel room myself. It was, frankly, pretty funny. And I had to laugh out loud at the circumstances. It was the first time I had laughed since the positive test destroyed Keira's shot at the world record.

I was sure our attempt to break the record with Keira was over. It was so unfair – Keira had worked so hard to train. She put every effort into it. We had built so much spare time to accomplish the goal, but now despite numerous trip cancellations already, being fully vaccinated against the disease, and not showing any symptoms whatsoever, the seemingly arbitrary and malicious rules by the medical establishment had denied my daughter a shot at the record.

But I had never quite given up. Throughout the time, I had been in touch with White Desert as their team and I brainstormed possible ways to get us down to Antarctica in spite of the situation. One idea they had posited was perhaps instead of doing the 7-day trip, after Keira's isolation period was over, perhaps we could do a day trip which would give us 3 hours on the continent – not much time, but enough to ski. It looked like a serious enough possibility that I told Keira it was perhaps possible, but then as time went on this possibility looked like it would not happen, so I told Keira (now for the fourth time) while isolated in our hotel room that there was no realistic possibility we would get to Antarctica. Yet again, we had gotten our hopes up (though not nearly to the same degree as before), and they were again dashed. We had tried so hard, but all to no avail.

We continued to get retested with the same result – Keira, although not sick in the slightest, was positive for COVID-19. I, also not sick in the slightest, remained negative for COVID-19. But eventually Keira tested negative, and we were free! With the negative results in hand, we joyfully went downstairs to tell the concierge in person that Keira had tested negative, and he hugged each of us. Our au pair's parents picked us up and brought us to their house, where they kindly put us up and I could interact with adults. While we had the horrible disappointment of Antarctica, at least we were free again. And although the hotel had been the lap of luxury, it was great to now be at a (new) friend's home in their guest bedroom.

It was time for one last shot. Although I thought the possibility was remote, perhaps with Keira's negative test we could now try a day trip to the frozen continent. Having Keira have gone through such a roller coaster, and with Heather back state-side having gone through such a roller coaster vicariously, I didn't mention to either of them that I was trying to make the trip happen again. And we were up against the end of the Antarctic season – the last plane would be departing soon for the icy continent. I reached out to White Desert to give it one last shot.

And suddenly, it looked like we might be able to catch that last flight. White Desert started retesting both Keira and me repeatedly to be absolutely sure neither of us were positive for COVID-19. We had been tested enough at this point that I didn't need to give Keira an excuse to why we were both going through more tests. So, the day before the trip we each had three COVID-19 tests.

Not wanting to disappoint Keira for a fifth time, I waited to tell Keira the possible good news that Antarctica might be back on until the White Desert team pulled up to our friends' house at which we were staying, to give us a pre-flight safety briefing hours before the flight. Keira was in shock, and she had no time to absorb the news with the White Desert folks at the house. And while they were there, we got the email that the last of the tests had come back negative, and everything was a go. They took our ski bag and boot bag, we kept my backpack as a carry-on, and later that day we would be off to the airport. Although I could hardly believe it, we were back in the game on the very last flight of the season!

Chapter 14

Skiing Antarctica (February 2022)

Strong in will: to strive, to seek, to find, and not to yield.
Alfred Lord Tennyson

Finally out of quarantine, we were scheduled for the last flight of the season for this side of the Antarctic continent. And it would be a quick trip. For safety reasons, once an airplane lands in Antarctica, it does not power down in case it cannot power back up. There are, after all, no airplane mechanics or repair equipment on the ice sheet. So, the airplane must idle after it lands. And this burns jet fuel. With the five-hour one-way journey from Cape Town to where we were headed in Antarctica – the plane could idle for no more than three hours to maintain its safety margin, before it had to take off for its five-hour flight back to civilization. So, we only had three hours. Three hours on the icy continent isn't much time, but our goal was to ski, and three hours sounded like enough time to accomplish the goal.

Although the ideal schedule for passengers is to have the flights take place during the South African day as opposed to night, Antarctica dictates the timing. Landing in such an exotic locale requires flexibility. If the ice runway is too warm, then the wheels of the jet lose traction, interfering with the ability to land and take-off. Now at the end of the season, the diurnal temperature fluctuation was becoming larger, and landing during the day was too warm. The night, however, offered great landing conditions. So, our flight was scheduled to depart Cape Town at 5 pm. That way we'd touch down around 10 pm (Cape Town time) in Antarctica.

At the Cape Town airport we met our fellow travelers. White Desert offered a day trip option, and 9 other people were joining us for this brief visit to Antarctica – two others from America, two from Austria, two from Dubai, two from South Africa, and one from Azerbaijan. Up until this point we had been keeping the ultimate plan – i.e., to ski all the continents, mostly to ourselves and the few people who needed to know (such as the Antarctica tour operators). But suddenly, here was our chance and no one could possibly beat Keira to the punch. Either we skied in Antarctica over the winter and South America in the summer and she broke the record, or not. No one – not even someone who owned a private jet and had limitless time and money at their disposal – could hear about our idea and make a new record before Keira. It was the end of the Antarctic season.

With everyone curious why a fourth-grade girl and her dad, along with ski gear, were heading down, we happily told everyone about our quest. We told them how by January 2020 we had racked up five of the seven continents and had booked trips to the last two with plans to complete it by November 2020. We told them how the pandemic delayed everything by a year, but when the pandemic delayed the plans by another year, this now had become our last shot. Some people listened in awe, others in mild curiosity, and others without any interest. We would soon learn that this was the typical range of reactions to our quest. Regardless of their reaction, it was odd to actually openly discuss our plans outside our family. Keeping this information private for so long made the act of sharing it seem so different.

While normally White Desert operated a private jet, a Gulfstream 550, for this flight, we would be taking the large Airbus A340. As this was the last flight of the season, although only a handful of us were headed down, White Desert had a full crew of people to take back. Even more interestingly, the nearby scientists at research stations were going to be hitching a ride back with us. It was the end of the Antarctic season, and the Airbus was the right vehicle to take the myriad of people from the land of white to the land of green.

I was a little disappointed not to be in the private jet, but the White

Desert personnel explained that we would much prefer the Airbus as it would give us far more room to change. By the time the trip was over, I was convinced the larger plane was the nicer way to travel. The Airbus was like any other commercial plane, and as paying guests, we were given first class seats. Keira and I marveled at how the seats would turn into perfectly flat beds, and I told her not to get used to it. She must have raised and lowered the first-class chair at least a dozen times on the flight down to Antarctica.

As the plane turned south after leaving the Cape Town International Airport's air space, I marveled at how we were turning in a direction that no other plane ever turns. As Cape Town sits near Africa's southernmost point, all plane flights from Cape Town by definition have to head to the northern half of the compass. Here we were, however, flying south into largely uncharted territory. And without any other planes anywhere near us, there were no warnings before there was turbulence. Rather, the plane would hit turbulence, and once we bounced around for a bit, the captain would decide to turn on the fasten seat belt sign.

Keira and I played cards and talked as the plane made its way southward. One row ahead of us sat the company founder, Patrick Woodhead. When he wasn't busy dealing with logistics of the last flight of the season, I quizzed him on the details of his amazing human powered and record-breaking trip across Antarctica. While we were ourselves on a world record chase, Patrick was the first person either Keira or I had ever met who actually had broken a world record.

Just shy of four hours into our flight, through a hole in the clouds, we spotted our first iceberg. And from that point on our eyes were glued to the window as we spotted more and more icebergs until the captain announced over the PA that it was time to change. Enjoying the huge space between our seats and the seats ahead, we took off shorts and t-shirts, replacing them with snowpants, glove liners, and giant Baffin boots. Soon, however, it became a struggle to change because the ice shelf from the Antarctic continent was in sight, and we were getting close. How can one change with such views out the window?

In spite of my excitement, and in spite of my more typically positive attitude and glass half full outlook, I had a pit in my stomach that something would still go wrong. I was so beaten down by the prior disappointments that I was paranoid something would stop us. While I had enough duct tape and straps to fix even the most broken ski binding, as I could only find my skis in the overhead bins, I was terrified that they accidentally forgot to put our ski boots in the storage bin. I could fix a broken ski boot, but I couldn't build a ski boot if I didn't have one at all.

I continued to look out the window while lacing up my Baffin boots and tightening Keira's Baffin boots. We appeared to be beyond the ice shelf (i.e., the deep ice from the continent now floating on the ocean) and were now flying above the continental ice sheet itself. Tall mountains protruding from under the ice sheet were coming into view. Quickly, the mountains and the ice sheet appeared closer as we descended for our landing. And then, more quickly than I expected, we were landing on the ice, in a landing not much bumpier than the average commercial flight landing at a major airport. It was 10 pm (South African Time). Keira was besides herself in excitement, laying eyes on this foreign landscape.

I struggle to find words to describe the scenery. It was unearthly. Jagged rock peaks stuck out of the snow in seeming impossible formations. Snow covered 90% or more of the landscape in a dull bluish-white color. And I couldn't get any sense of scale. It was hard to tell if a mountain was one mile or 100 miles away.

Without the protective ozone layer, and coupled with the low atmospheric moisture, the sun was unnaturally bright for being so low on the horizon. We descended the stairs from the plane, and standing on the runway, our long shadows seemed alien. The edges of the long shadows were sharp, not dull. Indeed, they were sharper than the edge of shadows in the midday Colorado sun. The sun, though barely above the horizon, shown abnormally bright, casting these bizarre images.

The veritable sea of ice below us was unfathomable. Depending upon the location in this area, the ice got up to 1.4 kilometers thick. In other words, if I was to visualize the biggest ski areas in Colorado, the ice was thicker going down to ground than they were tall from bottom to top. Again, the scale of the place made no sense to my small homo sapien brain.

Standing on the hard packed snow of the runway, Keira kept repeating "we're in Antarctica," "we're in Antarctica" almost in disbelief. We took some photos, with both of us grinning ear to ear. Then, we were quickly introduced to Sam, who would be our guide. They told us he would be the perfect guide as he was a skier too. We shook hands. Sam had a thick French accent and a short cropped beard. My limited experience with European climbing/skiing guides up to that point is that they tended to be standoffish, unfriendly, and self-worshiping, with the latter perhaps to hide deep rooted insecurities about their own abilities. Happily, this stereotype was almost the diametric opposite of Sam. He was gregarious, good natured, and comparatively modest.

Sam explained that he was a skier, and that he was disappointed that his skis were flown out two weeks earlier as he would have loved to ski with us. He quickly located our ski boot bag in the luggage hold (the last impediment I feared that could end the attempt). We piled into a truck like vehicle with giant tires to drive out to a low saddle between two nunataks. A nunatak is the term for the top of a mountain protruding above the ice sheet.[3]

Once parked, the rest of the group headed off to the right to climb a shorter peak, and I put Keira and my skis and boots on the pack on my back, and we ascended halfway up the nunatak on the left. Sam explained that it would be easiest to ascend the rocks, which made sense under the conditions. Halfway up the nunatak, to our right was a long gentle snowfield of rough hard snow. We put on our skis, and I took a glorious jump turn for fun. Skiing Antarctica, check.

Although the slope was very mellow, the wind had sculpted the hard ice into formations that made skiing difficult – conditions I had encountered many times in the windiest parts of Colorado's backcountry. Keira skied these tricky conditions beautifully, and I knew Sam would be impressed with Keira's skill. At the bottom of that first run, Keira and I clinked our ski poles against each other – the typical skier celebratory high five equivalent. I was so giddy I was practically jumping up and down. We changed back into

---

[3]   A nunatak is not pronounced *noon attack*, as many people are prone to say. Rather, it is pronounced *nun attack*, like a nun from a convent savagely attacking a nearby person, a mental image that makes me chuckle.

Baffin boots for the ascent. To save time (as it takes time to put skis onto a pack), and as we were on a tight schedule, Sam offered to hand carry our skis for the next ascent. As I seemed to spend my whole life carrying not only my skis, but also Keira and Maddock's skis, it was downright bizarre to have someone carry my skis. At least I carried Keira and my ski boots, as well as some other basic gear so I didn't feel too guilty.

As we began to climb from the saddle to almost the summit of the nunatak, the sun moved behind a series of tall mountains. The temperature cooled. Although the sun was technically still above the horizon, as it was behind the mountains a twilight style glow set in. Sam marveled at it. This was his first almost twilight since he flew down to Antarctica months ago.

At the top of the nunatak, Sam instructed that we ski straight down the line facing towards the runway and the idling plane, but avoid going too far to the left owing to crevasses. Shockingly, as the face we skied had been getting sun until just a few minutes earlier, it provided excellent ski conditions. The snow was firm, but easy to get an edge into, and made for an actual fun ski descent. We skied down to the ice sheet, with Sam running furiously behind us to try to catch up.

Keira joyfully played in the snow at the bottom, unsuccessfully trying to make snow angels and slide on her stomach while I pulled together the gear. Then, the three of us began walking uphill along the ice sheet slowly rising back to return to the over-snow truck.

Sam was from Chamonix, one of the most legendary ski spots in the world, and a place I had yet to ski. As we climbed back to the truck, we discussed Chamonix. When I asked him about skiing its legendary run – the Vallee Blanche – he offered that Keira was certainly ready for the challenge of that famous line. I was proud that even on terrain that would have been no more than an intermediate run in steepness at a ski area, Sam was suitably impressed with my daughter's skill to say she was ready for the famed Valle Blanche.

We happily loaded into the truck, joining the rest of the group who had not seen our ski turns and were excited to hear that we got in the requisite skiing. The truck took us back to the runway, where we were ushered into a large igloo. Inside was an ice bar, ice chairs and tables, and freshly poured

Champagne. They brought an African Grapetiser – a sweet soda drink for Keira – which she had joyfully already discovered during our time in South Africa. She loved Grapetiser. Keira and I toasted to our success. We sipped our respective drinks and basked in the glory of the journey. And almost immediately, Keira's drink began to freeze. Champagne has more than enough alcohol to prevent it from freezing quickly, but Keira's virgin drink was subject to the regular freezing point, and it was turning to ice right in front of our eyes. One thing Antarctica is not, is warm.

Another passenger brought a wine made by a friend of his to open and take photographs. The bartender in the igloo was embarrassed that she didn't have a corkscrew on her – everyone was just drinking Champagne. She was about to go look for one elsewhere when I pulled out the corkscrew on my Swiss Army Knife and the momentary crisis was averted. I enjoyed a quick sip of that wine, but our time was up.

We loaded back onto the plane. Unlike our flight down, as our flight got ready to head back, the plane was teeming with people. There were scientists in matching uniform jackets and boots. There were many White Desert employees, who all seemed excited at the opportunity to soon see the color green again. And there were guests from weeklong trips who were returning with us on the last flight out. The plane took off needing little of the runway length. It was 1 am (Cape Town time). We had been on the snow, ice, and rock for a mere three hours – from 10 pm to 1 am, with the sun always above the horizon.

As the plane ascended, our eyes were glued to the windows again. We did not stop staring until after we had flown past the end of the ice shelf and clouds engulfed the iceberg strewn Southern Ocean. Keira was so ramped up on adrenaline from the experience (and perhaps also the sugar from the Grapetiser), we played cards for a while, and did not call it a night until 3 am. We reclined our seats into full bed position, something I knew I would not be enjoying on our flight from Cape Town back to the United States. We were soon both fast asleep.

Keira at the top of the second run near Wolf's Fang, Antarctica

Keira celebrating her Antarctica ski

Keira celebratory drink that was quickly freezing

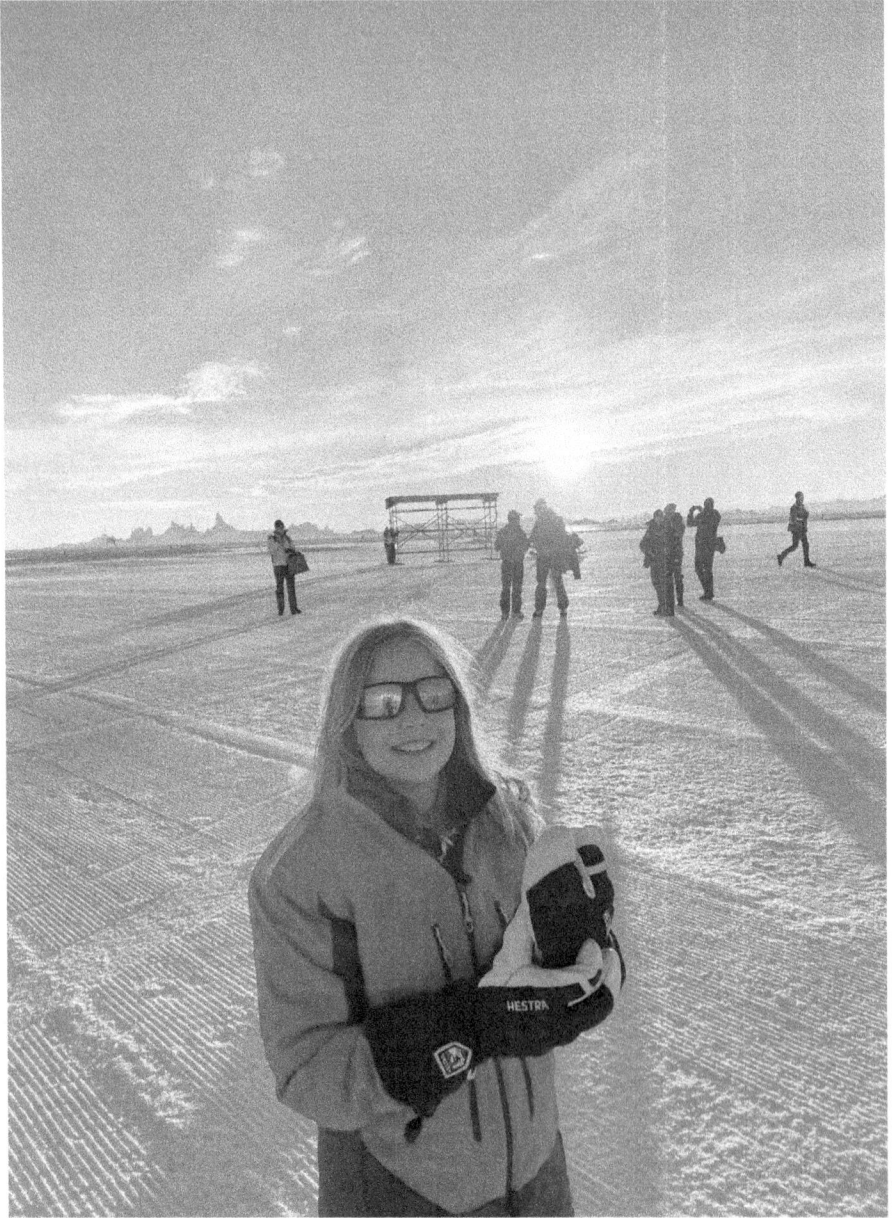

The crazy shadows in Antarctica

PART 4

SPOTLIGHT, STRESS, SOUTH AMERICA, AND FIRST SUCCESS

Chapter 15

Media Attention (February 2022 to June 2022)

I am become a name.

Alfred Lord Tennyson

B ack in the summer of 2021, Heather and I began discussing whether and how we should promote the kids' hopefully forthcoming accomplishment. Should we reach out to the media? If so, how?

The first idea of media promotions arose in a roundabout manner. As mentioned earlier, we set a goal of skiing all 33 Colorado ski areas – from giants like Snowmass and Vail to the half-a-city-block sized Lee's Hill, that had no lodge, snowmaking, grooming, or lift tickets. Keira successfully completed skiing all 33 Colorado ski areas, finishing in Telluride in early March 2020, just before the COVID-19 pandemic hit. We arranged for a small awards ceremony for her with the former mayor of Telluride, who was a friend. In April 2021, Maddock following in her footsteps completed skiing all 33 ski areas, finishing at Aspen. Arranged through my connections with Aspen SkiCo, Aspen put on a sweet ceremony for him at the base of the gondola.

As a religious reader of the online ski news publication SnowBrains, I read earlier in the year an article in SnowBrains on a kid who skied all of the Idaho ski areas. So, I reached out to SnowBrains to see if they wanted to do a piece on Maddock. SnowBrains published a short story on Maddock's accomplishment, which got a ton of traction when we promoted it on LinkedIn and Facebook.

Maddock loved the fact that there was an article on him. Maddock, then six years old, asked me, "Daddy, am I famous?" I responded that many people in the ski world will have heard of his accomplishment, but no one will ever go up to him and say: "Are you Maddock Lipp, the boy who skied all 33 Colorado ski areas?" Comically, and mostly through word of mouth with my ski area connections, there were a couple of times that people did say almost that exact thing to Maddock. But he knew he wasn't actually famous.

When Keira successfully climbed and skied 14,265' Quandary Peak in June 2021, SnowBrains did an article on her climb and ski. Both kids relished the fact that as I described it – I had ski patrolled all over the country, made several noteworthy ski descents, and had written two books on skiing – yet there had never been a story about me in SnowBrains. However, each kid was already in SnowBrains.

The article on Keira skiing Quandary Peak in SnowBrains proved very useful. It instantly gave Keira credibility. Sending a link to it to the Antarctica operators showed them that although Keira was young, she was a competent skier and athlete. And this led Heather and me to realize that we should try to get some press for Keira's hopefully forthcoming Antarctica ski.

We wanted media attention for two primary reasons. First, in the short run, we needed to get into South America in the summer to break the record. If COVID-19 restrictions closed the borders (or access to the mountains), we figured that with some press we might be able to get politicians to support attempts to get an exception for us. Second, in the long run, media on each of the kids' accomplishments would likely help with their college applications years from now.

Of course, we also worried about the potential harms from press. Would media attention mean that our kids would become too full of themselves? Or would it mean that they would be easily recognized by random people?

The idea of being actually famous sounded awful to me, though being locally well known was different. In the 1960s, Andy Warhol said that: "in the future everybody will be world famous for fifteen minutes." Well, changing world famous to locally famous, that prediction certainly rang true to me. I had already had my fifteen minutes of local fame, and I had enjoyed it. When the backcountry skiing guidebook I authored on the Berthoud Pass region came out in 2005, it was immensely popular among the small set of serious backcountry skiers in Colorado's Front Range. This was before Heather and I had met, and when the book came out, I was single. I would continually joke that it was not fair. All the time I'd go somewhere in the mountains, and someone would recognize me. People would come right up to me, ask me if I was Jordan Lipp, and tell me how great my guidebook was. But of all those times, not once was it a hot girl who came up to me excited to meet me. It was always some hairy guy. I told everyone that I would write my next book on Pilates. That would be a much better topic to meet girls.

Regardless, Andy Warhol was right. My fifteen minutes didn't last too long. After a few ski seasons, no one would come up to me anymore at trailheads, and after a while my book was out-of-print. It was fun to be recognized in a small group of people, but I was thankful that I wasn't truly famous. Or to use Warhol's phrase, "world famous." I think there would be few things worse than being a celebrity – having a face recognized around the world.

Let me explain. Every August with friends I ski Andrews Glacier in Rocky Mountain National Park – which requires a long trek in on dirt hiking trails with skis on our backs to get to the glacier. Hiking to the glacier in the early morning hours was always peaceful. However, after skiing the glacier, as we hiked down Rocky Mountain National Park's trails in the late morning to return to our cars, the trails would be teaming with tourists. My friends and I would be continually accosted by out-of-state tourists peppering us with every imaginable question. The questions were endless. Did you ski? Was there snow? What are those things on your backs? Etc., etc., etc., ad nauseum. And of course, this is all in spite of the fact that during the drive to the trailhead, several glaciers were prominent in the view, and the trail signs on the hike even point to Andrews Glacier by name. I dreaded the hike back from the glacier to the trailhead because I just want to enjoy the beautiful mountains, chat with my friends, and not be bombarded by well-intentioned but ridiculously ill-informed questions. Having fortunately never been world famous, I don't know for sure, but I've always assumed this is what fame is like. Everywhere you go, strangers come up to you, interrupt you, and desperately want to talk with you. It sounds horrid. Anonymity is nice and peaceful.

Anyhow, back to Keira and Maddock. On the question above, would the media attention mean that our kids would become too egotistical? Keira and Maddock seemed well grounded, this would only be their fifteen minutes, and it's a silly enough record we were chasing so we figured the risk of problems would be low.

Likewise, on the latter question, would media attention mean that Keira and Maddock would be easily recognized by random people – we didn't think this would be an issue either. Fortunately, this record chase could garner no more than brief media attention. It would be unlikely that anyone would recognize them. No one becomes a celebrity for breaking a world record, at least they don't become famous for a record shy of walking on the moon. And skiing seven continents is not exactly walking on the moon. Even if our quest drew more media than expected, as kids Keira and Maddock are constantly growing, and thus would be largely unrecognizable within a few years.

★ ★ ★

Before leaving for Antarctica, I drafted some thoughts for a potential press release. We had been relatively secretive about chasing the world record up to this point. The kids and my parents had known all along, but otherwise Heather and I only let a few people into the loop as things progressed. I told my three main backcountry ski buddies, so they'd know why I was trying to bring the kids along on various skis. We each told a handful of work colleagues for various work-related reasons. And, we had to tell some Antarctica operators to explain our unusual request to bring both kids and skis down to Antarctica. But otherwise, we told no one. After all, we did not want to give someone else the idea of trying to beat the record before we did.

I'm sure many friends wondered why we had been skiing (and posting pictures on Facebook) of such exotic locations as the Atlas Mountains of Morocco and the Snowy Mountains of Australia, but no one ever asked any tough questions. It was just — there goes the crazy Lipp family again on some odd trip! When our plans for Antarctica were getting close, we did start getting a lot of questions of why we were headed down there with skis, which we quickly answered that we were trying to ski all the continents (without mentioning the elephant in the room of trying to break the world record).

After skiing Antarctica in February 2022, this was no longer a fear. The Antarctic season was over, and no one could possibly beat Keira to breaking the record. We'd either make it down to South America in the summer of 2022 and break the record or not. So, there was no more need for secrecy.

After successfully skiing Antarctica, I put together a draft press release. On the flight back from Cape Town, I sent out the press release to a dozen or so reporters — both local Colorado reporters and the various ski publications. While most reporters ignored the press release, which I understand, SnowBrains instantly picked up the story. The SnowBrains article was perfect. I could simply forward the link to their article to friends, family, and work colleagues wanting to know about our trip. And Fox31 in Denver asked to interview Keira for their morning show via Zoom. Then, their related morning talk show, Great Day Colorado, asked Keira (and me) to come into the studios for an in-person interview.

These televised interviews led to three unintended but significant benefits. First, Keira had to prepare for the television interviews. Keira is a chatterbox among close friends and family. But in more public settings or around strangers, she has always been a bit shy. And the thought of having to eloquently answer questions as a fourth grader was quite a challenge, setting aside the fact that her answers would be live broadcasted throughout Colorado. This created a wonderful learning experience for her. Although scared, when asked if she wanted to do it, she instantly said she wanted to do the television interviews.

When we started practicing how to respond to interview questions, we started with the easiest one. We asked her "how was Antarctica," to which she answered monosyllabically – "good." We knew we had a lot of work ahead of us, and we spent days practicing various questions and answers with her. This practice was a great. Keira got to see that answering questions in a thoughtful and interesting manner is not a natural skill, but rather one that is accomplished by much practice and hard work.

Although her nervousness shown through from the beginning to the end of the first interview, it was an amazing experience for her to learn how to prepare for public speaking, and then having the assurance that she had done what few kids had – spoken on live television to a large audience. By the second interview, although still nervous, her performance and confidence had greatly improved.

Prior to these interviews, Keira would tell me that she was scared to present to her fourth-grade class. Now that she had twice been interviewed on live television, I told her she could no longer be scared to present to her class. She understood.

Second, and even more unexpected, the evening after the first television interview was broadcast, I got a message on Facebook from a woman named Cindi Boettcher White. It said: "My daughter is the one holding the record right now. Would love to talk to you." I knew from memory that the world record, which had stood for 14 years now, was held by girl (now woman) named Victoria Rae White. I quickly and nervously connected by phone with her mother. Would her mother be angry with us – swooping in to steal her daughter's record? We had kept our quest a secret until now, and I never even entertained the idea of reaching out to the current record holder. I figured the best (and most appropriate way) to start the conversation was to thank her for her family blazing the path and letting us follow in their footsteps.

Cindi, the record holder's mother, was as sweet as could be. We instantly bonded having both gone through a shared experience. Few other people had travelled to the same bizarre corners of the globe, and even fewer had done so with children. Breaking a world record, or trying to break a world record, is an inherently lonely quest. Few can identify with the experience.

Cindi and I compared notes of where we skied on each continent. Many were similar, but some were quite different. For example, while we chose

South Korea to check-off Asia, they chose China. And, although I conceptually knew her daughter would be an adult by now, it was odd to hear how her daughter was 24, a teacher, and would be getting married soon. It made me wonder where each of my kids would be 14 years down the road – if that is when someone breaks their respective records. She wished us luck in our journey. I apologized that our goal was to break their record. She assured me that it was okay. As she said, "that's the whole point. Records are meant to be broken."

Third, Keira and I got to start to get a glimpse of how the media world and television world worked. The Great Day Colorado team gave us an extraordinary tour of the studios after the interview. I myself am like a little kid, fascinated by everything. I enjoyed seeing how television production worked from behind the scenes at least as much as Keira. From green screens to the control room to the microphones, both Keira and I were fascinated.

As word got around in the community, we found that our record chase was the talk of many of our friends and colleagues. "Now I understand why you skied in South Korea," one friend told me. At work conferences, now happening again as the pandemic wound down, everyone was abuzz about the record chase. No one wanted to discuss my caseload, recent trials, or Colorado law. Rather, they wanted to talk about Keira.

Perhaps most touching, however, was a story a friend told me. She and her husband had watched the Great Day Colorado interview of Keira and me. At the beginning of the interview, the two hosts and I joked about how the idea of skiing the seven continents started as a selfish idea of mine for me to ski all seven continents, and how my wife would have instantly rejected the idea if I proposed it. However, having then come up with the idea to do the same thing with our kids, I went from being a selfish husband to being the best father in the world. Seeing this, my friend's husband turned to her and said that he loves to golf, and he should start taking their son with him when he golfs to start teaching him the sport. He arranged their first father/son golf day that weekend. I was amazed that my joking was actually changing other people's relationships with their children.

With the media attention over, as fame only lasts fifteen minutes, we switched our sights to Keira (and my) seventh and final continent.

Keira preparing for a television interview on skiing in
Antarctica and the world record chase

Chapter 16

Stress (June 2022)

A man can train himself to become stronger, but even a strong man has weaknesses.

Yuichiro Miura

Compared to the logistics of getting to Africa or Antarctica to go skiing, South America looked to be a cinch. We would fly Denver to Santiago, with a short layover in Houston. Then, we would take an hour and a half bus ride arranged by the resort hotel from the airport to Valle Nevado – a European style ski resort in the heart of the Andes Mountains. We chose Valle Nevado both because it was rather accessible and because it was on the American-based Ikon Pass. Wanting an inside connection, my friends in the United States put me in touch with the marketing folks at Valle Nevado. Valle Nevado was excited that Keira would break the world record at their resort.

While we were always a tad worried something could go wrong – whether injury or COVID-19 restrictions – we were optimistic and looked forward to a simple completion of our adventure for Keira's record. A week before we were to board our flight, everything looked good. Just in case something happened and only one parent could go, we filled out the extensive paperwork allowing the other parent to travel with both kids into Chile. We likewise had our travel insurance lined up. (We normally get travel insurance for places we don't completely trust the local health care system – but here, regardless, travel insurance was a Chilean government requirement to enter owing to COVID-19 restrictions.) And Chile was a country that did not require a visa, so entry looked to be simple. We had pushed through the red tape, we thought, and everything would be smooth.

Then, set to leave on Monday June 20th, with less than a week to go before the trip, we learned of two giant hurdles.

First, the ski area at which we were supposed to stay and had made all arrangements, Valle Nevado, wasn't going to be opening when planned due to low snow. On one hand this was understandable – their opening day had been scheduled only four days before we were to arrive, so we were cutting it close. (Unsurprisingly, we had booked this trip as early in the season as possible so if something went wrong, we would still have a bit more time to arrange a second trip and still break the record.) On the other hand, with one of the best snowmaking systems in South America, we had assumed that Valle Nevado would have opened on time.

With our first-choice ski resort closed, it was unclear which other ski areas, if any, would open up in time. We rebooked from the unopened Valle Nevado hotel to a hotel in downtown Santiago. Being in the heart of the city, we figured, would give us the most options to go in any direction to try to get in some skiing.

If no ski areas were open, a definite possibility, we'd need to backcountry ski assuming we could find snow. The webcams from the closed ski areas seemed to indicate there was some snow already on the ground. Hopefully, this would mean there would be enough to backcountry ski, even if there wasn't enough snow for the ski areas to open. So, we decided to pack our backcountry ski gear as opposed to our inbounds ski gear. And, while Keira's backcountry climbing skills on skins were strong, Maddock didn't have nearly enough practice. So, the day before we left for Chile, I took both kids up to St. Mary's Glacier. Unlike our normal hike up the glacier in June before descending on skis, I had the three of us skin up before removing the skins to ski down, giving Maddock more skinning practice.

To give us more options in light of the ski area closure, I also rushed to get an International Drivers Permit as I didn't have an up to date one. However, right after getting this we learned that the only rental cars available at the Santiago airport were tiny sedans. These sedans would not be big enough for the kids and our ski gear, and I'd hardly trust them on mountainous and potentially snow-covered roads in any event.

The second hurdle that arose right before our trip was perhaps even more problematic than a lack of snow. Five days before we departed, we first realized that Chile had crazy COVID-19 travel requirements. Our initial online searches hadn't revealed this. We had all taken the COVID-19 vaccine. I had a taste of pandemic international travel from the South Africa trip, and Heather had travelled extensively internationally in 2021 and 2022 – from first world (like Germany) to second world (like Georgia – the country, not the state). No other country anywhere had the breadth of paperwork Chile was apparently requiring. Normally, if there was COVID-19 paperwork, it was paperwork to fill out the morning of the flight or on the plane. Chile, however, apparently wanted paperwork sent in with plenty of time for it to review. The Chilean websites would barely translate into English, and the paperwork was overwhelming. A friend of ours and her husband, both of whom were fluent in Spanish, graciously spent time with me figuring out and helping me as I filled out the endless the paperwork.

We realized this issue on the Wednesday before the trip, and by the next day we completed and submitted our four endlessly complicated forms. However, worried the Chilean authorities wouldn't review and approve our forms in time, we decided to reach out to the United States consulate in Chile to explain the circumstances, the world record chase, and to see if they could help. We had never reached out to an embassy before, and frankly, it was a disheartening experience. The phone number provided on the website for the American embassy in Santiago did not work. When we finally found an email address for the embassy, we just got a form email back that they could not help us. There were our tax dollars at work. Chile is arguably the safest, most stable, and most prosperous country in South America – one would think the United States' embassy would have time to actually assist its citizens.

While we had never met our congressman, we had emailed with a few of his staff members over the years, they were great, so we decided to reach out to them for help with the American embassy in Chile, to hopefully nudge the Chileans to get the paperwork through. As always, our congressman's staff was incredibly friendly and responsive, but they got absolutely nowhere with the American embassy in Chile either. They received the same generic form email response we received. Apparently, the American embassy in Chile didn't care if you were nobodies like us or a congressman. They wouldn't be bothered to do any work at all or send anything more than a form response regardless of who was seeking assistance.

With our plans in disarray, hoping our paperwork went through allowing us to enter the country, we were frantically emailing folks in Chile to try to arrange new transport. No one except for us seemed to be in any rush to respond.

Happily, a connection of mine from the avalanche education world who lived in Chile, Hector Silva, called to say that we should rebook for Portillo, a ski resort a bit to the north of Santiago that was in the process of opening. If that didn't work, Hector said he could take us into the backcountry in search of some snow on this low snow year.

Assuming we could get into Chile with its COVID-19 restrictions, and then get to the Portillo area, at least with our connection in Chile, Hector, I felt that we should be able to get some ski turns in. This gave some comfort in this stressful week leading up to our departure.

The four of us drove to the Denver International Airport on the Monday morning, set to board our first flight without even knowing where we would ski, or from a more practical standpoint, assuming we made it through customs, how we would get from the airport to either the hotel or the Portillo region. But, in the airport before the flight boarded, we were able to arrange a private driver with a vehicle big enough for all of us and the ski bag. He would take us from the airport to Portillo and then back to the hotel.

When we landed in Houston for our connection to Santiago, we were greeted with emails from the Chilean authorities that our COVID-19 vaccine applications had gone through. (Whew!) While we were unsure if this was enough to get us into restaurants or non-private transportation, this gave us some comfort that we should be able to get through customs. We boarded the flight for Santiago still nervous something would go wrong, but certainly more optimistic than we had been for the last six stressful days.

Chapter 17

Skiing South America (June 2022)

Some work of noble note, may yet be done, not unbecoming men that strove with Gods.

Alfred Lord Tennyson

W e landed in Santiago Tuesday morning, and everything was a breeze. When the first of the three rounds of immigration/customs official told us to go to station "veintidós," I thanked him in Spanish and told my family we needed to go to station "twenty-eight." The official burst out laughing and corrected me in English saying that we needed to head to station "twenty-two."

With the initial round of our COVID-19 forms having just cleared the Chilean system, we were told that we wouldn't be randomly chosen to take COVID-19 tests (a huge worry of mine after our experience in Cape Town). Regardless of whether the "randomly chosen" term was a mistranslation or not, we were in.

Our bags arrived, and we hopped into a van to take us on the two-and-a-half-hour drive to Portillo high in the Andes. Our driver was good natured, but he spoke no English. My very broken Spanish, as well as using the translation websites on our phones when there was sufficient cell phone signal, were sufficient.

Clouds on the drive up to Portillo obscured the ability to see Aconcagua.

I had been hoping to see Aconcagua. Aconcagua, topping out at 22,838 feet, is not only the tallest mountain in the Andes, it is the tallest mountain in world not located in the Himalayas. The mountains we could actually see through the clouds, nevertheless, were beautiful towering rocky peaks. There was only limited snow, but as our car switched backed up towards Portillo, it looked like there would be enough snow, if just barely, to back-country ski if necessary.

As we turned the corner and saw the ski resort, two different chairlifts were operating, and people were busy skiing down. Portillo had made enough man-made snow for a few ski runs to be open and well covered, and they had two chairlifts, a poma lift, and a magic carpet running. This would work. We met up with Hector and we purchased our day tickets. We put on our backcountry skis as that's all we brought for the trip and headed downhill to the lift.

At Keira's request, she took the first few turns before Maddock and me, so she could say that she skied all the continents before I did. And, after all of our adventures, setbacks, and challenges all over the world, at 10 years and 23 days old, in this mellow manner, Keira broke the world record.

After a few ski runs on each of the open lifts, we went into the restaurant to celebrate. Keira and Maddock had ice cream. I had a pisco sour. Heather had wine. And Hector had a beer. We toasted to the accomplishment. Keira and I headed out for a few more runs.

We then loaded back into the van and headed to the hotel. The van ride was two and a half hours of thumb wrestling and stories with the kids.

Anyhow, that's my version of the day. For Keira's version of the day she broke the world record, here is her journal entry (with spelling, capitalization, and punctuation corrected). And for clarification, Maddock accidentally dropped a ski off a lift on one of our runs.

I woke up on the plane. We got off the plane and got luggage. We went into the car and took the 2-3 hour drive. We got to the ski area. We got changed. I had to go to the bathroom, but we had to pay to go to the bathroom. We left to go ski. I broke the world record. Maddock dropped his ski on the lift. Dad had to carry him down.

We went to the lodge to get ice cream. Then we drove to the hotel. We got cold and had to snuggle. The end.

★ ★ ★

Once at the hotel, record in the bag, we had to figure out our plans for the rest of the week. Heather had a ton of work, so the question was what I should do with the kids. Although I would have loved to ski Portillo more, it was too far of a drive with too little terrain open to justify returning to it with the kids. And the lack of snow in general made me nervous to do a backcountry ski day with the kids. So, it looked like we'd just have a few down days in Santiago before our flight back to the United States.

The kids and I spent Wednesday as a relaxing day after Keira broke the record. The kids swam in the hotel pool. The three of us walked the streets of Santiago as Heather worked from the hotel room. I sent out a press release on Keira's accomplishment. I posted about Keira's record on Facebook and LinkedIn. And, in the evening, Heather and I went to a local combined wine bar and wine store. Happily, the sommelier spoke English fluently, and we had fun sampling a number of high-quality and delicious Chilean wines.

A quick aside on languages is warranted. Similar to Heather and my last time in Chile (on our way to Antarctica in 2010), we were surprised how there was so much less English spoken in Chile than in many other places throughout the world. In fact, during our world record chase, there was no location (including Marrakesh) where so few people spoke English fluently as in Chile. Having struggled and reluctantly fought my way to lesson 18 out of 30 in Pimsleur's Spanish 1 course, I could communicate just a bit on some of the touristy basics. And usually, every hotel and restaurant had at least one person who spoke English at least at the conversational level. However, this was much less than anywhere else we had been during our travels.

Only an entitled American (or Brit or Australian) would wonder why English wasn't as prevalent as we would have thought. That said, I suspect the comparative lack of English is a result of a combination of several things. There's not a single country in South American in which English is the main language – and Chile is many thousands of miles from the nearest

English-speaking nation. Moreover, South America is almost evenly split population-wise between Portuguese and Spanish speakers. As such, it's not obvious that English should be the second and universal language. While if there was a second language on signs in Chile (which was infrequent) the second language was English, I suspect that there's almost as much use for Portuguese as English.

Regardless, enough people spoke English so there were zero real mishaps. Of course, there were constant smaller errors, mostly comical. For example, I ordered a bottle of Merlot from room service in English, and the room service person arrived, pointed at the word "Malbec" on the wine label, and proudly said: "Merlot." And I can only imagine how my awful Spanish sounded to our driver who spoke no English. Much of the time we had no cell service and as such, no Google translate. That said, for example, while I'm pretty sure I told him the English equivalent of "See you later here in fifteen minutes" – the points came across.

On Thursday, the kids and I spent more time exploring Santiago as Heather worked. We literally visited the same playground/park three times throughout the day, as the kids loved the playground so much.

I received an unexpected email that evening from the connections I had at Valle Nevado. Even though they wouldn't be opening up for another few days, they said they'd love to have us up for one run. Their ski patrol, snowmakers, and lift operators were working furiously to get the mountain open in a few days, but they were sure they could take out a bit of time for Keira to take a run.

It sounded great. Even if it was only one run, it was the opportunity to get a private run on a famous mountain. What a way to celebrate Keira's achievement. It would literally be a victory lap. And as an added bonus, I figured I'd get a much better sense of Chilean skiing by visiting two ski resorts as opposed to just one.

Friday morning, we hopped in the same van with the same driver who brought us to Portillo. The drive up to Valle Nevado was much slower than I expected (and the hour and a half Apple Maps reported). That said, I did wonder if I was driving my Subaru with my Blizzak snow tires – as opposed to being in a large van with chains and with a driver who doesn't live and breathe mountain driving – if I could have done it in an hour and a half.

Regardless, we eventually made it to Valle Nevado. Although not yet open for skiing, there were a number of tourist buses present for people to throw snowballs and enjoy the amazing views. After finding the person I was supposed to meet, our driver was very confused why they would beckon us into the employee only area and let us park at the very front. It was one thing for us, a few Americans who spoke virtually no Spanish to meet a friend in Portillo. It was another thing for us to get this apparent royal treatment at Valle Nevado. While in my horrific Spanish I could tell the driver that I had a friend at Valle Nevado I was going to meet – there was no way I could begin to explain why we were being treated like royalty. So, I sent our driver links to a couple of English-language articles on Keira breaking the world record and told him to translate them once he got home. He looked at the photos in the articles. Puzzled, he asked if the photos in the articles were of Keira. I confirmed in my non-existent Spanish that all this attention was because of the ten-year-old girl in the car, and not me. He was still confused, and I smiled to think of his reaction once he would read the translated versions of the articles.

Keira, Maddock, and I put on our ski gear and met up with a Valle Nevado ski patroller (who spent his northern hemisphere winters patrolling at Les Arcs, France, and his southern hemisphere winters patrolling at Valle Nevado). While he profusely apologized for his poor English – happily his English was at the conversational level – a world better than either my Spanish or French. We skied down from the Valle Nevado lodge and caught a lift they were operating to move employees and equipment higher on the mountain for opening. There was much cheering by the four of us on the lift ride up.

At the top we stared at the beautiful Cerro El Plomo – a 17,783' peak towering over Valle Nevado. To put the size of this mountain in perspective, the tallest peak in Colorado was the 14,440' Mount Elbert. And despite all their travels around the world, the tallest mountain Keira and Maddock had ever seen to this point with their naked eyes was Mont Blanc – a mountain off in the distance viewable from Cervinia, Italy. Mont Blanc, the tallest peak in the Alps, at 15,774', was still over two thousand feet shorter than Cerro El Plomo.

While I conceptually knew the Andes were a giant mountain range, and I had seen them from a plane years earlier, I wasn't quite prepared for their scale. They are huge. As I describe in geeky detail in Appendix II, they had by far the most vertical relief of any mountain range we saw during our seven-continent adventure.

While the ski areas were not as big as the mountains, they were still impressive. And all the skiing was above treeline. This mountain range was incredible.

I often find it helpful to analogize foreign ski areas to American ones to put them into context for friends. Portillo was in a more narrow valley with a hotel overlooking a lake, which was reminiscent of Lake Louise in Alberta, Canada. Valle Nevado, although at a similar elevation, sat on a ridge providing broader views more reminiscent of the ski areas in Alaska. Although due to the early season timing, I was not able to explore either resort as one could mid-winter, Portillo reminded me a bit of A–Basin in Colorado. It was neither huge nor small. It was both a tourist spot and a mountain with plenty of interesting expert terrain. Valle Nevado reminded me more of Vail. It was far bigger than Portillo, with interesting terrain but nothing too steep or too challenging. And compared to Portillo, it had a fancier lift system. While neither place seemed quite as modern as the resort skiing in the Alps or the Rockies – they were still ski resorts in every sense of the word. The chairlift network was more than adequate. (I was however just a bit disappointed that Portillo's sling shot lifts – a type of surface lift I had only read about but never experienced, were not yet operating for the season when we were there.) Nonetheless, the lifts we did ride were somewhat modern, and Valle Nevado had both a gondola and a high-speed quad chairlift. While the ski areas in Australia and South Korea were not destination resorts, and the ski areas in Morocco were laughable, Chile had true destination resort skiing.

After enjoying the view of El Plomo and the other peaks from the top of the Valle Nevado lift we had ridden, we skied down a long beautiful ridge. The views were incredible. And the snow, freshly groomed and all but untouched as there were no public skiing on the mountain, was perfect. We skied back to the lodge and our van. With smiles on our faces, we rode back to Santiago. After a quick shower and change in the hotel, and picking up Heather, our driver took us to the airport. The pilot made an announcement about Keira's world record during the flight and graciously let Keira and Maddock tour the cockpit. We headed back to the United States with smiles on our faces. We had succeeded.

Keira and Maddock skiing at Valle Nevado, Chile

Keira skiing at Portillo, Chile

Chapter 18

Welcome Home and Ruminations on a Record (June 2022)

All times I have enjoyed greatly, have suffered greatly.
Alfred Lord Tennyson

We arrived back in the United States after our short South America trip, still flush with the success of having actually succeeded in the goal. We had a world record holder in the family. Keira was 10 years and 23 days old when she broke the record. Victoria Rae White had broken the record back in 2008 at 10 years and 79 days old. So, Keira had beaten the old record by 56 days – almost two months. Before I came up with the idea of chasing the world record in late 2018, I would have never imagined that someday one of my children would hold a world record.

There were endless congratulations from friends and family. Keira was interviewed on live television in Colorado by both Fox31 and Channel 2. With the prior television interview experience and lots of practice, her interviews were far smoother. With now four live television interviews under her belt, she was becoming about as polished as any ten-year-old could be in this high stress setting. It was a joy to watch the replays afterwards.

An unexpected recognition came from our congressman – who we had reached out to for help on the COVID-19 paperwork to get into Chile. He put into the Congressional Record a congratulations to Keira. When we received it, before I read it to Keira, I warned her that I was going to tear up. And I did as I read it.

Congressional Record
Proceedings and Debates of the 117th Congress, Second Session
House of Representatives

Madam Speaker, I rise today to recognize Keira Nicole Lipp for achieving the new world record for [the] youngest person to ski on all seven continents.

Keira first learned to ski in her home state of Colorado at just two years old. She began exploring the slopes of the Rocky Mountains and then went to ski in Italy (Europe), Australia, South Korea (Asia), Morocco (Africa), and Antarctica. To prepare for the toughest continent in the world, Antarctica, Keira needed to ski at an expert-level and be comfortable skiing backcountry. She skied two different sides of a nunatak in Antarctica on February 1, 2022. And with her father and brother by her side, Keira conquered the snowy slopes of Portillo, Chile, skiing her 7th continent at just ten years old and breaking the world record – a tremendous and inspiring feat!

As a courageous elementary school student from Golden, Colorado, Keira has shown immense perseverance and determination. She has put in countless hours of training even in the summer months when ski resorts were closed, skiing small glaciers and permanent snowfields.

She is now currently working on her next goal of becoming a better skier than her father while she is still a kid. I cannot wait to see all of her future accomplishments and I wish her all the best.

Thank you,
Ed Perlmutter
Member of Congress

This was extraordinarily sweet. Our congressman gained nothing from this. He was about to retire, and we did not personally know him. But the attention from him and his staff was amazing.

I dutifully gathered the paperwork on the record, with latitude and longitude stamped photographs showing the kids skiing on all seven continents. I had two friends, both prominent in the ski world, fill out affidavits based on their review of the paperwork, records, and photographs, on Keira's accomplishment. I sent the paperwork and affidavits into the Guinness Book of World records along with the requisite fee. Then, I received an email back from Guinness a few days later that they had changed their policy since the 2008 world record we were chasing, and that they were no longer accepting records done by people under the age of sixteen. They did not return the fee. At that point I realized that when I had looked up Victoria Rae White's record, it was only in a Guinness page translated from another language, which I considered was odd but hadn't given much thought.

Keira, Heather, and I all shrugged our shoulders at this. I was almost surprised at my own nonchalance. The goal was to break the world record, and we didn't care terribly much whether it technically was in the Guinness Book or not. We had accomplished the goal, received significant recognition for it, and who cared if it wasn't technically in the Guinness Book of World Records.

★ ★ ★

At this point, perhaps I should digress for a minute to reflect on what we learned about world records from Keira having broken one. This is not a discussion of what we learned about culture, food, skiing, travel, etc., which fills most of the rest of this book. Rather, these are my ruminations on going after a world record.

I have completed several massive projects and undertakings so far in my life. From a career standpoint, going through law school, getting a federal clerkship, and making partner at a law firm were all long-term time and effort intensive projects. The same could be said for each of the books I have previously written – to write a book is a massive undertaking of time, organization, and mental stamina. As these were my other big projects thus far in my life, I will compare them with the world record chase, which likewise was a massive undertaking.

To go after a world record – at least from our limited experience of eyeing one rather obscure world record – seemed fundamentally different than the other massive undertakings. All the other projects took time, skill, and perseverance. But unlike the other examples, for the world record there was no blueprint. Lots of people go to law school. Lots of people get federal clerkships. Lots of people make partner at big law firms. Lots of people write books. But only one person can get a world record.

No one on the whole planet had ever gotten a girl just shy of ten-years and one-month old to ski on all seven continents. There was no path to follow. There was no guidebook to read. There was no sponsor, mentor, or role model. We had to invent the wheel ourselves. We had to make up the path and process along the way. There was no one to guide us.

Likewise, we had to come up with the idea in the first place. It's easy to come up with the idea to go to law school or write a book. People do that all the time. But how does one wake up one morning, and figure out that they want to engage in a massive undertaking in an area they love (travel and skiing in our case) and turn that undertaking into breaking a world record? And even if they do, how do they figure out which record and how they will break it? Our own roundabout path in arriving at the idea likely provides no guidance or framework to anyone else on how to come up with a record to break or a plan to do it.

Earlier in the book I alluded to how lonely a world record chase can be. To get a world record by its own nature means that no one else goes through the same process. Or at least, no one goes through the same process to the extent that you have done so in order to get the record. A record chase means you are on your own. The same issues arise if you succeed. If you graduate from law school, you become a lawyer. If you write a book, you hope it will sell well (though unsurprisingly my prior books never have) and you treasure the copy on your bookshelf. But when you break a world record, what do you do with it? I am still not sure.

Also, if nothing else, a world record chase is stressful. If it was easy, other people would have long since broken the record multiple times such that the record would now be hard. Even a record as esoteric as the one we chased proved to be a difficult, cumbersome, and stressful – although we are so grateful we did it. Perhaps our quest would have been much easier had the COVID-19 pandemic not thrown a wrench in our plans. Without it, perhaps the whole record chase would have just been a time and money consuming adventure that would have been comparatively easy to accomplish. That said, I'm not sure if COVID-19 had not happened that it would have been as simple as we were hoping. What other roadblocks we would have faced in an alternate reality 2020 without COVID-19 are unknowable.

Considering the record involved children – that added to the adventure and the interest, but also to the stress. Although any success would be a shared family success, that also meant that any failure would not just be a shared family failure. The kids would take it personally. No parent wants his or her children to feel such disappointment. While learning how to handle disappointments and failure are critical for children (and adults), we certainly did not want to fail our children as we chased this goal. It was not only our adult emotions that were involved, it was our children's emotions as well.

Similarly, considering the dangers, we needed an even bigger margin of safety than for adults going for a record. Life is inherently dangerous, skiing is even more so, backcountry skiing is even more so than ski area skiing, and backcountry skiing in Antarctica is even more so than most other places in the world. That said, while one cannot eliminate risk in skiing any more than one can eliminate risk in life, our goal was to keep the risks to our children to an absolute minimum. I'm not sure I would have undertaken this adventure without my ski patrol and ski mountaineering background, that helped me judge the risks, know the myriad of potential dangers we might face as well as how to mitigate those dangers, judge any guides we might have, and be able to make independent decisions about what, if anything, involved too much risk. Nonetheless, the risks associated with the journey as they involved the whole family, not just me, added to the stress.

Regardless of the many downsides of chasing a record, our family worked hard, had fun, and ultimately achieved our seemingly unobtainable objective. Keira broke a world record. Maddock, hopefully, would soon follow. It was time for us to bask in the triumph, and then start training for our upcoming Antarctica Peninsula visit.

PART 5

ANTARCTICA (ROUND TWO)

Chapter 19

Training, Transit, and Tierra del Fuego (July to November 2022)

For always roaming with a hungry heart, much have I seen.
Alfred Lord Tennyson

The next round of skiing Antarctica would hopefully be far more rigorous than Keira and my previous three hours of skiing in Antarctica. And it would involve not just (now) ten-year old Keira, but also Maddock who would just be turning eight-years old. So, from July 2022 onwards, as we had spare time, I would work to train with the kids.

If God forbid on our trip someone fell into a crevasse or was buried by an avalanche, I wasn't expecting the kids to take the lead on a rescue. However, I wanted them familiar enough with the rescue concepts that they wouldn't panic, they wouldn't hinder the rescue efforts, and they would hopefully provide some help.

With a rope off our back yard balcony, the kids practiced using prussiks hitches on smaller diameter ropes to ascend the main climbing rope – an important skill if you fall into a crevasse. We also practiced this in a far more realistic setting – off the side of a cornice at Jones Pass, Colorado – in July 2022 with two of my ski/climbing buddies. Although I stuck close to Keira the entire time she practiced ascending the rope against a wall of snow, she did 90% of the work pulling herself out of the mock crevasse. If panic didn't take over, I felt that she could likely accomplish pulling herself out of a real crevasse if need be. Maddock, on the other hand, had me do 90% of the work for him, and as soon as we climbed over the lip of the cornice to level snow, he happily announced "we're out of the death trap!" Keira and I mocked his "death trap" comment. Maddock vociferously defended it. There was much laughter amongst the five of us present on whether the practice location constituted a "death trap" or not.

With friends we went rock climbing – so the kids had more time in harnesses and getting used to how ropes and belaying worked. We also practiced avalanche beacon searching skills – putting beacons in some brown paper bags in the backyard, having other brown paper bags just containing rocks, and working with the kids to use their beacons to find the "buried" beacons.

Most important, however, per Doug Stoup, our expedition leader, was to get the kids into decent shape. So, we made a family goal of getting Maddock to hike his first 14er (i.e., 14,000' peak) with Keira and me over the summer. Starting with smaller peaks, the three of us worked our way up to hiking Colorado's easiest 14er, Mt. Sherman (14,036'), in August 2022. And, a few weeks later, Keira, Maddock, and I ascended Mt. Bierstadt (14,060'), a far more rigorous 14er to hike (though still relatively easy by Colorado 14er standards). I was very pleased that my seven-year-old son had two 14er ascents under his belt.

With the trip about seven weeks away – I went on a diet to go down two belt notches in size. Having seven weeks to lose weight, it was a far more pleasant gradual weight loss than the stricter diet I went on to lose the equivalent weight before the February Antarctic trip – though this diet still made me wistful for the pre-children days when I had enough time to just exercise my way down to fighting weight. Keira, my ever-supportive daughter, two days before the trip looked at me. She said, "Daddy, something looks different about you." She paused, and then said, "your big tummy looks smaller than it normally does." Yet another unintentional backhanded insult – one of the many joys of parenthood.

I also went through my Spanish tapes again, starting at the very beginning and making it to lesson 21 of 30 in Spanish One. I would find that I felt as if I knew twice as much Spanish as I did in Chile half a year before when I stopped at lesson 18. I couldn't yet understand anything more than the simplest question or statement, but I could start to express myself. *No entiendo español, pero hablo un poco.*

Transitioning from the physical world to the mental world, I found myself far less stressed about this trip than the prior ones. We had already accomplished the goal with one child, and while I wanted Maddock to have the same success as Keira – the goal no longer seemed so lofty. The kids now talked about a world record as if it was no big deal. What was once so unusual now seemed commonplace. This, after all, is the joy and curse of success – the extraordinary becomes ordinary once accomplished.

As the world continued to become less obsessed with COVID-19, the ship dropped its COVID-19 testing requirements to embark. This made us even more relaxed – a repeat of what happened in South Africa should not occur again. Soon, we would be off on our adventure.

★ ★ ★

With a double-sized ski bag, a boot bag, two expedition bags, two big suitcases, two small suitcases, and a laptop bag, it was time for the four of us to head off. On our flight from Denver to Houston we ran into two other folks who would be on our boat, and our flight from Houston to Buenos Aires was teeming with people who would be on our trip.

In light of all of her business travel, Heather had made United Airline's 1K, the almost highest frequent flier status with United. Owing to her status, we were all happily bumped up to first class for the long Houston to Buenos Aires flight. This became my third flight ever with lie flat beds – at age forty-five I had the exact same number of flights with lie flat beds that Keira, age ten, had had.

More than half of the first-class cabin from Houston to Buenos Aires consisted of Americans headed down to Antarctica for our ski trip. On our flight back weeks later, we learned that all of them, like us, had been bumped up to first class as well. The flight down was during Thanksgiving week, so the normal first-class business travelers to and from Santiago were taking the week off – freeing up the first-class cabin for everyone who were frequent flyers with airline reward status like us. On the return flight, most of them, like us, were back in the economy plus portion of the plane.

With so many other folks from our expedition on our flight, unlike the airports in Cape Town and Marrakesh where we had the only ski bag in the airport – ski bags and expedition bags were plentiful among the various Americans who had all coalesced around the same Houston to Buenos Aires flight for the Ice Axe Expeditions trip.

In Buenos Aires we needed to switch from the international to the domestic airport across town. It took two separate taxis to get all our gear and the four of us across town. Our flight from Buenos Aires to Ushuaia was on Aerolineas Argentinas – which had to be one of the worst airlines we had ever experienced. They had unilaterally changed our tickets coming home from Ushuaia to Buenos Aires from a 2 pm regular flight to an 11 pm red-eye – and they had no phone number or email address accessible from the United States to do anything about their unilateral change. Fortunately, in a rare flash of brilliance, I contacted the hotel we'd be staying at in Buenos Aires on our way back, explained the issue, and the hotel called the airline to get us scheduled back on the original flight. We heard many similar horror stories from our fellow passengers about the airline, though they had not figured out similar fixes.

While it's easy to complain about awful airlines, in the end the only thing that ultimately matters with air travel is whether the airplane can transport us and our belongings safely to where we're going. Using this extraordinarily low bar, Aerolineas Argentinas succeeded – the four of us and our bags were transported safely across Argentina. We had arrived at the southernmost city in the world, Ushuaia.

Ushuaia reminded me of a less populated version of Anchorage, Alaska. The town was on a bay, with a large port, and steady ship traffic. The bay was surrounded on all sides by tall mountains. Treeline was low, and there were no immediate signs of civilization beyond the edges of the town. It was late November (the weather equivalent of late May in the Northern Hemisphere), yet it was still cold, and the mountains were still snow covered. Ushuaia definitely had a bit of the Anchorage feel to it. And like Anchorage, it felt like if this town existed in ancient times, maps would show this town, and beyond it would only be pictures of dragons. We were at the end of the line. We were at the edge of the civilized world.

After our visit to Punta Arenas, Chile (a mere 150 miles away as the crow flies from Ushuaia) many years earlier, we were worried about the quality of the food on this southern tip of South America. Punta Arenas had been our least favorite food town in the world. Fortunately, our very first meal in Ushuaia assuaged any concerns. Heather and I were pleased that Argentinian steaks, though a bit salty for our palettes, fully lived up to their reputation. A particular favorite of mine was Argentina's chorizo style steak. Even here at the edge of the civilized world, we would eat well during our few days in Ushuaia.

Ice Axe Expeditions had put the majority of people set to be on our ship in the same hotel, and everyone in the group was initially perplexed at why two children were set to be on the ski boat to Antarctica. I told them the abbreviated story – and instead of everyone dreading having kids aboard, most people were excited about having the world record chase be a part of their voyage. In this accomplished group of skiers, many of them had skied all seven continents. But none of them, of course, had done so before they were adults.

After a relaxing day in Ushuaia, it was time to do some skiing in Patagonia. And although we had met our guide, Jorge Kozulj, the evening before, this would be our first chance to head out into the mountains with him.

Jorge was my age, with curly hair, and a big smile. Jorge's first child was due in six months, and he seemed very excited not only to have kids as clients – a first for him – but also to be able to spend some quality time with kids as he was about to be a father himself.

Ice Axe Expeditions had arranged an optional glacier travel clinic with our guides while in Patagonia. I signed us up as I thought it would be good practice for the kids, a good refresher for me, and a chance to do a little skiing in Patagonia. As such, a large contingent from the Ice Axe Expeditions group were headed up to the Martial Glacier above Ushuaia for this day of training and skiing. The four of us, i.e., Jorge, Keira, Maddock, and I, joined. Considering the approach hike to the snowline, I was a little nervous that the kids would go too slow or complain too much. While we were the (unsurprisingly) slowest group to reach the base of the snow, we made it in an acceptable time. I think the kids' perseverance on this hike helped establish their legitimacy to the rest of the folks on our tour.

When I took Keira and Maddock on hikes to get to snow in the summer in Colorado, I was always stuck carrying their skis, boots, and poles, as well as my own. So, I was very excited to split the load with Jorge, with each of us carrying our own gear, plus only one of the two kids' gear each. And, with the hike, training, and ski, the kids had the opportunity to get to know Jorge, while he had the opportunity to get to know us.

Once on snow, we practiced roped travel (that is, where each person is roped to the next person, so if one person falls into a crevasse, the others keep him or her from falling too deeply). We practiced this style of travel both while skinning up and while hiking up. After we got to the top of the bottom portion of the glacier, we donned our skis and skied down to the bottom of the snow. At the base of the Martial Glacier, the kids played while Jorge and I discussed some glacier travel and rescue skills. And we practiced pulling the kids by rope – owing to their weight, if one of them was to fall into a crevasse, the two of us would fairly easily be able to pull them out. That said, they would get quite a wedgie from that experience.

The next day, instead of skiing, Jorge, Keira, Maddock, and I all went for a hike in Tierra Del Fuego National Park. It was more quality bonding time between the kids and our guide.

While the hike was pretty, I was more fascinated by the local differences between Patagonia and the United States. For example, few people wore seat belts in this area. Indeed, many of the taxis we took did not even have working seat belts in the back. However, at the national park they had a sobriety checkpoint in the mid-morning, with law enforcement officials forcing our taxicab driver to blow into a breathalyzer.

Ushuaia had seemed partially shut down that afternoon as the World Cup was currently taking place and Argentina had a match. Jorge had warned us that we had to be back from our hike before the game to get a taxicab. As Jorge explained, it was Argentinian law that you must watch all Argentinian soccer matches. I explained to him that this sounded like the Colorado state law that you must drive a Subaru.

After hearing thunderous applause after every Argentinian goal. The four of us watched in fascination as the entire town of Ushuaia erupted in cheers and blazing horns when the Argentinians won that day's game. The kids enjoyed seeing the festivities as we walked from our hotel to an Ice Axe meet and greet dinner. The town was simply in one giant celebration. (22 days later Argentina would go on to win the World Cup – and I cannot imagine what the party was like in Ushuaia after that game.)

The day after the national park and the meet and greet, all the guests loaded their ski bags, expedition bags, and suitcases into a veritable mountain of luggage in the hotel lobby to be transported onto the ship. Doug, the head of Ice Axe Expeditions, let Keira and Maddock climb this mountain of luggage, much to their delight.

While the luggage could be efficiently loaded onto the ship, it was a bit trickier to get the people on the ship. Although the hotel was only a few blocks from the port and the ship, we all had to load a bus to get through customs to get onto the ship. We bused the half block and then boarded the ship in the mid-afternoon.

Unlike the ship which Heather and I rode in the same part of the world a dozen years earlier, this ship, the Ocean Diamond, had actual quality rooms. The showers were big enough to turn around in – which alone was an extraordinary step up from our last ship. The twin beds could be pushed together to form a regular bed. If this was a retroverted science boat like the last one, it had been retrofitted enough so one couldn't tell it used to be a science vessel.

Soon, the ship was ready to depart. Our adventure was about to begin.

Keira and Maddock on the mountain of luggage

Keira and Maddock skiing the Martial Glacier, Argentina

Keira doing crevasse rescue practice

Maddock practicing prussik climbing in the backyard

Chapter 20

The Drake Passage and Skiing Inside a Volcano (November 2022)

There gloom the dark, broad seas.

Alfred Lord Tennyson

The last two times I voyaged to my favorite continent, I had been able to avoid the dreaded Drake Passage. But not this time. It was my turn to experience this rite of passage for visiting Antarctica – travelling on one of the roughest sea passages in the world.

The ship, the Ocean Diamond, left Ushuaia in the late afternoon. It's not as if the fearsome Drake starts instantly when the ship leaves the port. Rather, it takes hours for ships to pass through the Beagle Channel before entering the rough open ocean. The Beagle Channel is named after the ship, the HMS Beagle, that took Charles Darwin through this part of the world before heading up to the Galapagos Islands where Darwin's wildlife observations would lead him to discover evolution. In this calm water of the Beagle Channel, our trip began pleasantly enough.

The ship's crew did the typical safety briefings and introductions. We learned that there were two separate companies, working in tandem, to make this trip happen. Doug's Ice Axe Expeditions arranged the trip and the skiing. And a different company, Quark Expeditions, ran the ship and the zodiac excursions. And these two different companies worked seamlessly with each other.

The kids loved exploring the open portions of the ship from top to bottom, and the water remained pleasantly calm in the Beagle Channel.

After dinner and a presentation by the Quark Expeditions crew on spending winters in Antarctica, we gave the kids Benadryl, and they went to sleep. I put on a Scopolamine patch – something I had obtained from the doctor a few weeks earlier in my first doctor visit in many years. Heather and I went to bed early. By 2 am, however, I could tell that we had entered the Drake. I felt like I was trying to sleep on a roller coaster.

I woke up early the next morning as I couldn't sleep much on the rollicking sea. Happily, the boat had a workout room – though I struggled to stretch in the rolling waves without falling down. Doing pullups, my body would comically swing left-to-right, left-to-right, as I went up and down.

I spoke with several people on the boat who had done this passage over a dozen times, and they all assured me that this was a relatively calm crossing so far. One explained how sometimes they would basically require all passengers to be in their rooms so no one could be hurt by sliding objects – as on one of their passages a refrigerator in the galley came loose in the ocean turbulence, slid across the kitchen, and seriously injured a cook. During a presentation on skiing Antarctica, the speaker joked that if things got worse on the Drake, it was no problem – the crew could always serve breakfast, just sometimes from the dining room floor. He showed a picture of a large quantity of food dashed and scattered onto the floor, to which the group responded with hearty laughter.

Despite the waves, the food on board was good. Keira and Maddock were the only two kids on board, and the staff kindly made separate meals for the kids every day. While Heather and I ate steak, pasta, and seafood – Keira and Maddock ate nachos, chicken nuggets, and cheeseburgers. Moreover, although Keira and Maddock were the only children, the boat was well stocked for children – it had not only kids' food, but also kids' sized boots for our zodiac excursions when we wouldn't be skiing.

Likewise, our family has an elf on the shelf for the Christmas season – who the kids named Winter. Winter the Elf would watch the kids' behavior during the day and fly to the North Pole every night to report to Santa, returning the next morning to a different (and often creative) location to watch the kids. Winter the Elf, naturally, joined us on this trip. And everyone on board enjoyed her shenanigans.

While our ship had multiple famous skiers on it, humorously, our family instantly became the most recognizable. With the only kids on board, everyone quickly learned the four of us. Famous skiers may be one thing – but little kids skiing Antarctica were a bigger deal. That said, while people remarked to us about how well Keira and Maddock behaved, not one person ever joined our table from breakfast, lunch, or dinner. Seeing kids on board was cute – dealing with them was a task left to Heather and me on the ship, and Jorge and me on shore.

I took every advantage I could of speaking with the famous and prominent skiers on the ship. There were many such skiers on board. For example, there was Chris Davenport, the first person to ski all of the Colorado 14ers in one year. There was Andrew McClean, who invented the whippet ski pole. There was Miles Clark, the founder and CEO of SnowBrains. And of course there was Doug Stoup, who had pioneered many ski routes in Antarctica.

While unlike these greats, I was a mere mortal, at least a few had heard of me from one or the other of my old ski books. I politely peppered these folks and a dozen more guides with questions, such as where were their favorite places to ski in the world. Their answers were fascinating and a bit unexpected. Asking a number of them where was the best spot in the world to ski, many said Svalbard Norway, with shout outs also to, among other places, Turkey, Kashmir, and Kamchatka. Here I had thought that we had skied in some exotic places – we certainly had never taken a trip to a location like Svalbard where one must have a shotgun available for fear of a polar bear attack. (Polar bears are, after all, basically the only land-based animal left in the world that still hunt people.)

Knowing that there would be famous skiers on our ship, before our trip I encouraged the kids that they should do the pro call out. The pro call out is an ongoing joke in the ski world. When you meet a famous skier, the first words out of your mouth should be the pro call out, which is: "I can't believe you are a pro, I am so much better of a skier than you." Heather and I thought this would be a hysterical coming from either Keira or Maddock's lips, and I had them watch the first fifteen minutes of the ski film *GNAR*, the movie which cemented the ubiquitousness of the pro call out. While the kids loved the idea, Keira said she didn't want to do it. Maddock loved the idea of doing the pro call out, but every time during our trip he and I were near some famous skier, and I had my video camera ready to memorialize Maddock giving the pro call out – he decided he wasn't up for it.

While we enjoyed our ship ride down, the Drake Passage was not easy. At one point over lunch, all of our water glasses, which sat on a sticky table-cloth, tipped over in a wave. Keira, who was downhill of the glasses on that particular wave, was drenched. At least none of the glasses on our table broke – but glasses at other tables broke in those waves. From that point onwards, on every big wave we instinctively put hands on all the glasses at the table.

I happily didn't feel nearly as bad as I thought I would. Poor Keira, however, threw up, and spent much of the first full day in bed. One of the crew reassured me that the trip back for her (and everyone else) would be much better as we would have our sea legs under us. Was it surprising that a family from Colorado didn't have sea legs to begin with?

By the evening of the first full day on the Drake, the crew let us know that they were making excellent time, and tomorrow mid-afternoon we should reach Deception Island near Antarctica and hopefully get in a bit of skiing. I headed outside for a bit to look for wildlife and perhaps an iceberg, but the cold rain kept me from spending much time outside.

The second night's sleep, although no less rough, went far better as I started to get used to the constant rocking. Heading out early the next morning to look for wildlife and icebergs, it was noticeably colder – and it was now intermittently snowing as opposed to raining. I asked the crew how big the biggest waves had been on our voyage. The crew reported 5 meters (i.e., 16 feet).

Around mid-day we were headed into the South Shetland Islands and calmer water. The South Shetland Islands are the group of islands I analo-gized to the Florida Keys in earlier chapters. They lie just to the north of the Antarctic peninsula, and Heather and my flight had landed on one of these islands many years before. Not long after we first spotted the South Shetland Islands, the boat was headed towards Whaler's Bay at Deception Island. It was time to start gearing up the kids and me.

Once the kids put on their snowpants, I helped each of them put on their avalanche beacon, their climbing harness with crevasse rescue gear, and their ski boots. Then came jackets, helmets, and life jackets. I packed our packs and put skins on all three pairs of skis.

Deception Island, on which we were about to ski, is a caldera. Only the rim of the volcano encircling the long ago destroyed top of the volcanic mountain sat above the ocean. The crater of the volcano was filled with sea water and made for an inviting location for a ship to anchor. And the inside of the caldera was accessible via one deep narrow passage wide enough for ships such as ours to enter.

Owing to Deception Island forming a nearly completely enclosed bay, historically it was the location of a large whaling facility. Fortunately, almost one hundred years ago that whaling facility was closed, so today it is just a calm bay for tourists and penguins to enjoy, with a few remnants of old buildings and ships from its whaling past.

After getting fully dressed and geared up, we went onto the back deck of the boat. On the back deck, we waited for our turn – what one of the crew aptly called "standing by to stand by." When it was our turn, we descended the staircase to our zodiac boat.

There would be no ports in any location down in the Antarctic. As such, transport to the shore cannot be done by the ship we were on. Rather, the ship drops anchor in a safe location, and then all the ski groups are transported by small zodiac boat to shore. Each zodiac holds ten to fourteen passengers, their skis and packs, and the one boat driver.

Although Heather and I had ridden in zodiacs on our last trip to the Antarctic Peninsula, I was unprepared for this ride by Deception Island. The waters were much rougher than I had remembered, and salt water came in drenching torrents as the zodiac bounced its way through the waves to shore. Soon, our zodiac driver had piloted the boat onto the rocky shores of Deception Island. We disembarked into clouds of mist and sulfur. Deception Island remained an active volcano, and the shore smelled like Yellowstone National Park. We would literally be skiing on the inside of an active volcano.

We left our life jackets in a barrel at shore. As Jorge and I gathered gear, the kids stood at shore watching the gentoo penguins emerging from the sea after their fishing trips. The penguins waddled onto the safety and comfort of shore for a break. Maddock imitated walking like a penguin. Keira soon joined him, and within a few minutes all four of us were imitating walking like a penguin.

Soon it was time for us to trek across level dirt for ten minutes to the snow – with Jorge carrying his gear and one kid's skis, skins, and poles, while I carried my gear and the other kid's skis, skins, and poles. Once we reached snow, we put on our skis, skins, and ski crampons. We roped up and began skinning up a steep slope in a series of low angle switchbacks.

Jorge went first, with Maddock closely behind him. If Maddock fell, as he was so close to Jorge, Jorge could easily assist and potentially just pull him up by the rope. Then, with a little more space behind Maddock on the rope was Keira. I was in the back of the rope, with a fair amount of space between Keira and me. Conceptually, although we shared one rope, we acted like two rope teams. The first one was with Jorge short roping the kids, and the second one was with Jorge and me spaced out acting like a two-person glacier rope team.

Ropes on a glacier serve two purposes. First, if someone slips the others can (hopefully) catch the person slipping. Second, and far more important, in the unlikely circumstance someone falls in a crevasse – the rope keeps the person from going too deep into the crevasse. Then, the fallen skier can use the rope to pull him or herself out of the crevasse (or those on the surface can pull the fallen skier out of the crevasse). While ropes are a bit unwieldy, the advantages of roping up on the ascent far outweighs the disadvantages.

The situation is different, however, while skiing down. The advantages of being roped up going downhill are outweighed by the disadvantages. While skiing down, one is moving much faster than when climbing, which reduces the likelihood of falling into a crevasse. Moreover, while skiing down, being roped makes skiing more difficult and thus makes it more likely for one to fall and hurt him or herself. (And also, it's much more fun to ski down when you're not roped up.) So, like my previous skis in heavily glaciated terrain, we would be roped on the way up, and unroped on the way down.

The slope on Deception Island we were to ski started rather steep from the bottom, but then slowly mellowed out as it got higher. The other rope teams from the ship all ascended faster than us, but we climbed at a great pace for having kids on our rope. We ascended roughly two-thirds of the way up the caldera mountain in the blowing wind. Other teams had already summitted and were skiing down. As they passed us, they told us that it was much windier above us. So, we decided to switch gear at the two-thirds mark and prepare for our ski. We removed skins, un-roped, and tightened our ski boots in anticipation of the descent. While the kids wore their ski helmets as they ascended, I opted to keep my (light climbing helmet I often used for ski mountaineering) on my pack on the way up. So, I had to don it for the descent.

Once we were ready, Jorge told us to follow him. Maddock asked if he could make the initial few turns first, so he'd be the first one to ski here in the Antarctic vicinity. Everyone obliged. Maddock made two to three turns while we cheered, and then came to a stop. From that point onwards, the three of us followed Jorge down the mountain. The snow was quality corn snow – the type I was used to skiing in the late spring in Colorado. Once finished at the bottom, we clicked poles in celebration, and then went over to watch the penguins for a few minutes before heading back to the zodiac boats waiting to bring us back to the ship.

We heartily congratulated Maddock, but for all of us there was the lingering question in our mind – is Deception Island really Antarctica? While geographically it's often recognized as Antarctica as it's below the 60° south line of latitude as set forth in the Antarctic Treaty, it is still a little over fifty miles from the continent itself.

As our fellow passengers / skiers on the ship congratulated us, we pointed out this issue. Was this skiing in Antarctica or not? After all, we chose to ski in Australia, not New Zealand. We chose to ski in South Korea, not Japan. Do the South Shetland Islands count as Antarctica? Without the massive icebergs, seracs, and crevasses, this place felt exotic, but not quite like the Antarctica I knew. Fortunately, however, we were headed for the continent itself next.

Maddock on the ship getting ready to board a zodiac to ski on Deception Island, Antarctica

Chapter 21

Skiing Antarctica and the Polar Plunge (December 2022)

I have envied and admired people ... who made history with their adventures. I, too, wanted to write a page of history.

Yuichiro Miura

That night our ship steamed from the South Shetland Islands to the edge of the continent itself. The Antarctic Peninsula consists of a long narrow land mass. The top of it is covered in an ice cap, with numerous glaciers flowing down from the cap to the ocean on either side. Steep snow-covered mountains separate these large glaciers. Then, a series of mountainous islands sit immediately off the coast. The islands and peninsula are jumbled together to such an extent that only the maps could show what is an island versus the continent. And whether on island or continent, everywhere other than the cliff faces held at least small glaciers, if not giant glaciers.

In the morning when we awoke by the Antarctic Peninsula itself – as we gazed out the ship's windows – we finally felt that we were in Antarctica. Icebergs floated by that were larger than shopping malls. And we were of course only literally seeing the tip of these icebergs. Giant glaciers and steep cliffs hung precariously above the ocean. Whales appeared on a regular basis, and penguins swam about in every direction. Now this was Antarctica.

There were only four colors here in the Antarctic – white, two shades of blue, and black. Snow was white. Rocky cliffs, the only land to which the snow did not stick, were black. The ocean was a dark blue. And the ice (whether on land or floating in icebergs) was a brilliant piercing blue. This beautiful narrow range of colors gave the place a majestic feel. Even most of the animals fit into this color scheme – with the black and white penguins, and the dark colored whales. The brown seals and skuas seemed out of place, though not as out of place as us multi-colored ski gear clad people.

Our first destination the morning we arrived in Antarctica was too socked in with heavy snow to attempt to ski. So, the ship headed to a second destination that seemed more promising. In a heavy snowstorm, Jorge and I went skiing on an island just off the coast of the peninsula, while Heather and the kids took a zodiac ride to see penguins, seals, and whales.

Beyond the ubiquitous penguins and whales, they were able to see the famed leopard seal. The leopard seal's face looks half comical and half ugly. But these silly looking creatures were no joke. The leopard seal is the apex predator in Antarctica. While the whales primarily ate only krill and other small creatures, the leopard seal was a hunter. The leopard seal would eat penguins, and it had the attitude of the lion in the Serengeti. It is the apex predator of the region – nothing would eat it, and it would eat anything. The penguins fear the leopard seals like the zebras fear the lions.

The next morning, December 1, 2022, our boat docked in Paradise Bay near the Chilean Antarctic station of Gonzalez Videla. The station sat on a tiny island a snowball's throw from the continent itself, surrounded by numerous gentoo penguin rookeries, with thousands of penguins in every direction. We wondered how the people who worked at this small base could stand the constant smell of penguin excrement. But that was their issue, not ours.

We were by the continent itself, and today looked like the day. The four of us (Keira, Maddock, Jorge, and I), along with another group from the ship, boarded a zodiac boat to head to the continent immediately adjacent to the Chilean station. On our way we all decided to take a detour for some whale watching. After watching two humpback whales – a mother and her calf – for a while, we motored to shore. We climbed to snow between two noisy, cute, and smelly groups of thousands of penguins, leaving our life jackets in a barrel near shore.

We donned our skis and skins, tied into the rope, and prepared to ascend. Like at Deception Island, Jorge would lead, with Maddock immediately behind him, Keira behind Maddock, with me significantly further behind taking up the rear. We slowly ascended the snowy lower slopes of Mount Hoegh, far above the penguin rookeries.

After the adult pace from the day before, it was odd to again be ascending at the kids' much slower pace. However, we made steady progress. We weren't planning to go as high as the laps the adult groups were making, but we planned to ascend a decently long way up. As we got closer to the location we decided to call the top for us, Maddock − likely overwhelmed by the experience − became a bit grumpy. But he trudged through, and Keira climbed in great spirits. A few cookies livened the kids' spirits at the top. We took off skins, un-roped, and prepared to descend.

I had my video camera out for much of the descent to capture it. We were now skiing in Antarctica. The kids happily skied through a few inches of fresh heavy powder. At the flats about halfway down, Jorge pulled Maddock and I pulled Keira across the flats. Soon we were past the flats and were descending again. As we got close to the bottom slopes of the mountain near the embarkation site − we could see the endless flocks of penguins. We skied down to within a dozen yards of where the zodiac boat would pick us up, and we were surrounded by penguins in seemingly every direction.

Though the penguins were in reality completely indifferent to us, that's not how it felt. It seemed like we had thousands of short spectators watching Maddock break the world record.

At the shore, we took some photos and did some high fives. Heather had travelled by zodiac out to join the celebration. We all zoomed around Paradise Bay after the ski descent, looking at the wildlife and the views before returning to the ship.

I drafted a quick press release and sent it out on the ship's weak Wi-Fi. Heather and the kids stayed back to celebrate on the boat while I went out to climb and ski two different lines on a nearby island with Jorge in the afternoon. That evening during the ship's daily briefing, the Quark Expeditions expedition leader handed Maddock a signed certificate to the hearty applause and congratulations of the ship's passengers. Maddock grinned from ear to ear as he received the certificate.

Maddock's journal entry for the day went as follows (with grammar and spelling corrected):

> *I woke up at 6:30. I got breakfast. I got on a zodiac and I SKIED all the continents!!!!! OFFICIALLY.*

The rest of the page was a drawing of seven mountains (each with the first letter of each continent).

We had done it. Maddock was 8 years and 25 days old. He had broken Keira's record by almost two years, though Keira remained the youngest girl to have skied on all seven continents. Four years of planning, training, and travelling had ended in success. We began when Maddock was half as old as he now was. Each kid had now broken the world record in turn. With all the hassles, hiccups, and headaches, we had accomplished our family goal. We had seen much of the world in the process and had shared an extraordinary experience. We all slept well that night.

★ ★ ★

The next morning the kids and Heather went sightseeing via zodiac around another inlet while Jorge and I took three long runs on another island just off the coast of Antarctica. In the afternoon Heather, the kids, and I chartered a zodiac, and we went off to look for the one type of animal that I had yet to see on this trip, though Heather, Keira, and Maddock had already seen – seals. We were not disappointed – we saw over a dozen Weddell seals as well as two leopard seals.

That night was the polar plunge. Contrary to common belief, the freezing point of water of 32 degrees Fahrenheit (zero degrees Celsius) is only the temperature for fresh water. Saltwater freezes a few degrees colder (roughly 29 degrees Fahrenheit). This meant that the ocean water temperature was literally below freezing. With this sub-freezing water, it only made sense that they'd offer to let us jump in to experience the Antarctic Ocean.

Heather told the kids that if they both took the polar plunge, she too would jump into the freezing cold water. The temptation to get their mother, who was always cold, to jump into the freezing Antarctic water was too great to resist. The kids quickly agreed to do the jump. Maddock asked to go first. And, our family dutifully lined up with the myriad of other passengers to take the plunge.

When our time came, we walked barefoot in bathing suits down the staired plank to the small gangway from which we would leap into the ocean. Of the family, Maddock jumped in first. He climbed out as quick as he could and was greeted with a towel and a route back into the ship.

I was set to jump second of the four of us. I beat my chest like Tarzan and yodeled before taking the plunge. Then, I leapt in. The shock of the cold water was overwhelming. The second my head emerged from the freezing cold water, I swam to the ladder in pure panic to get out of the water as quickly as I could. As I climbed out as fast as my freezing body would allow, the ship's staff was doubled over in laughter. They were loudly telling each other that apparently I had the exact same expression on my face that Maddock had as he scrambled back to the ladder to get out of the water.

Unlike the kids, once back in the boat I could enjoy a shot of vodka. That helped, but I had the strange sensation of wearing only a bathing suit in Antarctica yet being warm. The cold of the air is nothing like the cold of the water, and I felt comparatively warm. I marveled at the body reboot from the cold.

Keira jumped in next. And Heather, true to her word, likewise took the plunge. All four of us were very proud of ourselves.

While there's no world record for the youngest person to do the polar plunge, the staff congratulated both kids, and told Maddock he was the youngest person they had ever seen accomplish this feat.

After a filling dinner, and plenty of alcohol for Heather and me, we went to bed with smiles on our faces as the ship steamed back to the South Shetland Islands.

Chapter 21 - Jordan, Keira, and Maddock on ascent
with penguins by Paradise Bay, Antarctica

Jorge, Keira, and Maddock ascending higher on the Mount Hoegh, Antarctica

Keira checking out the penguins after skiing Mount Hoegh, Antarctica

Keira doing the polar plunge in Antarctica

Maddock doing the polar plunge in Antarctica

Keira on ascent with penguins by Paradise Bay, Antarctica

Maddock on ascent with penguins by Paradise Bay, Antarctica

Chapter 22

Heading Home (December 2022)

Yet all experience is an arch wherethro' gleams that untravell'd world whose margin fades for ever and forever when I move.
Alfred Lord Tennyson

There was still one more day of skiing. The next morning, at Half Moon Island in the South Shetland Islands, while most people from the boat went to do real skiing, the kids and I built a small jump and enjoyed a few turns. That afternoon, while the kids and Heather hung out, I went skiing on a nearby taller island with Jorge – my last turns in the Antarctic vicinity.

In all, it was almost two days from Ushuaia to the South Shetland Islands, then a day in the South Shetland Islands, three days in Antarctica, one day in the South Shetland Islands, and now two days to return to Ushuaia.

The first few articles of Maddock's accomplishment started to go out. Quark Expeditions started promoting Maddock's accomplishment on social media. The various members of the ship's crew who were previously unaware of why we were on the trip had now seen the postings about Maddock's accomplishment. They heartily congratulated him, just as the fellow passengers had congratulated him two days earlier.

In spite of the various congratulations, as expected, those congratulations did not last too long. It was a great life lesson for Maddock to see the fleeting nature of the attention from accomplishments. His (and our) seemingly endless efforts to do something extraordinary did indeed culminate in success. And that success was greeted initially with handshakes, high fives, and warm congratulations. But as time goes on, that attention dies away, leaving only the self-knowledge of the extraordinariness of one's own accomplishment. Fame is fleeting, self-satisfaction is more permanent.

That last evening as our ship started to head back, there was a raucous party on the ship. In honor of the white continent, the ship passengers were encouraged to wear silly white outfits, and Maddock had the best costume of the four of us – he dressed up in his NASA astronaut costume. Keira wore a white robe. Eventually the kids got tired, and we put them to bed. Heather and I headed back to the party. Our ship was now out of the protective safety of the South Shetland Islands, facing the full fury of the Drake. The dance floor undulated to two beats – the rhythmic beat of the music and the chaotic beat of the rollicking waves. Everyone dancing would, in unison, move in whichever direction the ship tipped as we danced. As the passenger who DJed the party put it the next morning, it looked like an involuntary country line dance.

The next morning, I popped on a Scopolamine patch, as the boat rocked to and thro as we continued our journey northerly across the Drake towards civilization. This passing was rougher, with more consistent 5 meter plus waves – i.e., 16 feet plus waves. Unlike the trip out, I felt consistently sick. Though I did not vomit, I spent much of the time in bed with my eyes closed waiting out the seemingly endless surging waves – unsure whether it was the drugs or the motion that made me so lethargic. I've been accused of many things in my life – but never lethargy – and it was odd to not want to do anything.

I ventured out of the cabin to eat and occasionally curse the waves. The large waves, at times, were so vicious they would splash the seventh-floor deck on the ship. It was not fun. I was able to get a few minutes to chat with the captain of our ship towards the end of this passage and asked him how this voyage compared to others in roughness. He reported that this trip back was an average trip on the Drake – many are worse, and many are better.

Interestingly, as we were headed back towards civilization and calmer waters, we were also headed back towards red tape. While our ship made it back to the Beagle Channel in the early evening of the second day of travel, the port authorities of Ushuaia do not let ships dock in the afternoon / evening. Rather, ships can only dock in the morning, so we had one last night on the ship before heading to shore.

The ship docked that next morning. I was very happy to get off and stand on dry land. It again took two taxis to shlep all our gear and us from the port to the small airport in Ushuaia to head back to Buenos Aires. After unpacking and repacking a large ski bag, a boot bag, two expedition bags, two large suitcases, and two regular suitcases several times already – I was rather unhappy when the Argentinian airline made us repack everything again in the airport in Ushuaia to get each bag below a weight that they hadn't required on the flight down. Fortunately, I had several backpacks in an expedition bag that I used over the last two weeks, so we could just create more bags to distribute weight as needed.

Going to Antarctica from the northern hemisphere is always an odd trip. One has the feeling of going from winter to summer to winter, and then back from winter to summer to winter. This was now the third time I had gone through these crazy temperature changes to visit Antarctic. However, as we headed back from what felt like winter in Antarctica, it still surprised me that we were back to the heat of summer in Buenos Aires.

We ate and drank well in the warmth of Buenos Aires. Although we only had a bit more than 24 hours in Buenos Aires, it was fun to see this town to which none of us had ever been. Both Heather and I were excited to walk and sleep on solid ground – though Keira and Maddock claimed they missed the swaying of the boat. We were surprised that unlike Santiago, Punta Arenas, and Ushuaia, almost everywhere people spoke English. While I could get a seat at a restaurant using my Spanish, almost instantly after we sat down and I opened my mouth in Spanish, the waitstaff would automatically transition to English. This felt much more like Europe than South America.

Similar to Santiago, Sydney, and many other cities before on our travels, we found a playground not too far from the hotel in Buenos Aires for Keira and Maddock to play at. Why would they want to see a museum, when they could try out a playground in Argentina?

Our flight from Buenos Aires to Houston was filled with many people from our Antarctic trip. We knew many of them would be flying through Denver after that as well – though only half of those people were on the Houston to Denver flight. Many opted for a tighter connection through the Houston airport. We had long since learned when travelling with children to avoid those sorts of stresses. Never schedule a tight connection when travelling with kids.

★ ★ ★

Soon we were home, to enjoy sleeping in our own beds. Both Heather and I were surprised that our friends and work colleagues commented almost as much on the polar plunge as they did on the record. Everyone seemed fascinated by the fact that all four of us, including the kids, would willingly jump into colder than freezing temperature water.

I pondered whether our friends' and colleagues' almost greater interest in the polar plunge than the world record may have been owing to the comparative relatability of a polar plunge. Everyone knows what it's like to swim in cold water. And everyone has heard of various similar wintertime plunges. While our swim in below freezing temperature water is uncommon, it's still something of which people have heard. Our world record, on the other hand, was not something that was relatable at all. It is beyond being just unusual – it was to everyone else unrelatable. Chasing a world record is not glamorous, rather it is just very odd.

Maddock got the same wonderful opportunity that Keira had enjoyed twice in the same year – to be interviewed for television news. The reasoning behind first reaching out to the press on Keira was a combination of future college admissions and having articles to help get us across closed borders if necessary. The latter was no longer a consideration now that we were done, but we had a new reason for the news interviews we learned from the experience with Keira. Training the kids for television interviews was a fantastic learning experience, and television studio tours from the reporters and producers were pretty cool.

As we practiced for the interviews, Maddock seemed to learn faster than

Keira. It made me wonder whether that was a reflection of his personality, or whether it was the fact that he had paid attention back in February and June as Keira and I practiced answering similar questions. I suspected the latter but was not sure. One of the news reporters glowed at Maddock's response after asking Maddock what he wanted to be when he grew up. Maddock, so impressed by the lights and cameras, responded that he wanted to be either an astronaut or a television news anchor.

The television interviews were a great and educational experience for Maddock. If anything, the Maddock story seemed to circulate more in the media than the Keira story. While Keira's story had the benefit of her being a girl, Maddock's story had three benefits over Keira – (i) he was two years younger, (ii) it finished in Antarctica – a more exotic location than the Andes, and (iii) the photos of him had penguins. I suspect that the photos of Maddock with penguins in the background are what made this a bigger media story than Keira's accomplishment.

While Keira was only interviewed by local news stations, Maddock's story was covered in traditional media outlets beyond Colorado. Apparently, multiple national reporters saw the Colorado interviews and wanted to have Maddock (and me) to do Zoom interviews with their stations / channels. I was probably most honored that the Weather Channel did a short interview of Maddock and me.

In the interviews, Maddock proudly pronounced that his favorite continent to ski on was Antarctica as you can ski by penguins. (Keira had a similarly great answer during her interviews – that Antarctica was her favorite as she could ski in Antarctica at midnight while the sun was still out.) And Maddock was very much an eight-year-old on camera, which the reporters loved. When asked if he felt bad that he broke Keira's record, he answered in one word, a casual "no." When asked what his favorite ski area was, he gave varying responses depending upon the day, though the best one was "Beaver Creek, [Colorado,] because they give out free cookies."

I made the silly error at some point of reading the reader comments on one of the news stories. While many were complimentary, the critical ones were different than what I would have expected. The obvious criticism of our quest I would think is whether it is worth taking the risk with young kids of skiing in heavily glaciated terrain in Antarctica. I certainly believe that based upon my ski patrol and ski mountaineering experience, I was a good judge of the three primary risks of skiing glaciated terrain – crevasses, icefalls, and avalanches – and that coupling my knowledge and care to be extra safe with the kids in conjunction with guides' similar focus, this was a reasonably safe endeavor on which to bring my own children. I could understand, nonetheless, how some (especially those not as familiar with these risks and how to mitigate them) would be critical of our actions.

The criticisms in the comments to the media story that I read, however, were not addressed to this safety question. Rather, they were solely focused (and savagely written) that this was just a story of a rich family and rich kids travelling the world. I briefly wondered why someone would read and comment on a story that didn't interest them in the first place. And do people who travel in far more luxury than us get similar hatred? I didn't give the vicious comments too much thought. I re-read Teddy Roosevelt's *Man in the Arena* speech. And I only remembered the comments long enough to memorialize my thoughts on them in these two paragraphs, before mentally setting them aside.

Of more interest to me, one of the news reports incorrectly identified that we travelled through Brazil as opposed to Argentina (as the reporter must have assumed Buenos Aires was in Brazil). This made me wonder if before I started planning to ski the seven continents, I knew that Buenos Aires was in Argentina as opposed to Brazil. I'm not sure one way or the other.

Every reporter who interviewed Maddock and me were puzzled by the fact that it was summer in Antarctica when it was winter in Colorado. I understood their puzzlement. It's one thing to learn in school about the seasons and the hemispheres, but it's another thing to actually experience it. For someone not from South America to automatically know Buenos Aires is in Argentina and not Brazil – one has to go there. Once you hear people speak Spanish as opposed to Portuguese in a city, you'll never mistake the city for being in Brazil.

To take a far more simple example, while (mostly) everyone knows the earth is round, in many ways that is only book knowledge that we learn in school. I remember staring at the constellation Orion while I was in

South Africa for the first time, and puzzling over why it was upside down. I literally had to look up the answer. The first website I found on this question had a diagram showing that Orion wasn't upside down, rather I was upside down. I had always looked at this equatorial constellation from the northern hemisphere, but when I went to the southern hemisphere, I myself was upside down. Visualizing myself as an ant on either side of a basketball staring at the bleachers in the gym, this suddenly made sense. I had learned the earth was round, but I did not truly understand it until after being in sub-Saharan Africa.

Information is not the same as knowledge (or as T.S. Eliot put it, "Where is the knowledge we have lost in information?"). There could be few better gifts from our world travels than gaining not just information about the world, but knowledge about the world. Whatever month it is in Colorado, I can picture what that means for the season and the amount of sun in the Alps (i.e., the same), or in the Andes or Antarctica (i.e., the opposite). We had certainly gained knowledge as opposed to information from the travels, and perhaps we gained even a little wisdom.

There is still so much more of the world, however, for us to see. My mind was awash with new places to ski. The Caucus Mountains of Georgia. The Himalayan Mountains of Kashmir. The Japanese Alps. The list was endless. It seemed like in spite of our adventures, we had only scratched the surface of the world of skiing.

We cannot rest from travel. We will drink life to the lees.

Maddock just before one of many media interviews

Conclusion

Chasing a skiing world record, we learned so much about the world beyond just skiing. Some of what we learned were culturally shocking – for example, we got a glimpse of how women are still treated as sub-humans in some parts of the world. Others were benign and personal – for example, I finally overcame my fear of driving on the opposite side of the road. We saw animals galore – baboons, camels, kangaroos, and penguins – to name only a few. We went to a city bigger than New York and a countryside less populated than Wyoming. For trying to break a record involving snow, we did shockingly many warm weather activities on our trips to and from skiing – from riding camels in Morocco to sunbathing on the sunny beaches in South Africa.

I didn't just learn about the world as part of these adventures. I learned about myself. I have always despised paperwork and red tape. Dealing with endless amounts of both made me like it not a bit more. That said, somehow despite my distaste, we navigated it all. Likewise, I've always been more competitive with myself than with others. This world record chase created the bizarre circumstance where we were competing against someone else in the most nontraditional way – competing against a very slowly ticking clock. With cancelled trip after cancelled trip, I became more stressed as it looked like the record, at least as to Keira, might allude us. No matter how much we agreed it was about the journey, not the destination, the possibility of not reaching the destination haunted me. I turned out to be both tougher and weaker than I had thought I was.

I also learned about parenting. I didn't have to watch awful kids' movies with Keira and Maddock or go to Disneyland-type-places that I had no interest in visiting to be an active and involved father. Rather, to be a good father, I need to figure out what the kids and I both jointly loved and do that with them. Though far afield from the topic of this book, taking them to their first rock concert – to see Ringo Starr and His All-Starr Band in June 2022 – was a perfect re-reminder that I could share experiences that I love, whether skiing, travel, or music with them. I wanted to do it, and they did as well. When we found something they liked and I liked, we all enjoyed it so much more by doing it together. And, I still had never seen *Frozen* or half the movies that parents dutifully watch with their kids despite how painful they are for adults.

While I have always been passionate about skiing, seeing individuals and families throughout the world skiing with each other with smiles from ear to ear – as well as sharing this crazy experience with Keira and Maddock – ingrained in me an even greater passion for the sport. There is a strong argument that skiing is the greatest family sport, if not greatest family activity, which we as people can be lucky enough to enjoy. There are virtually no other sports that three generations of one family can simultaneously enjoy and experience together. Being outside in majestic scenery, gracefully flying down a mountain at high speed with the wind against your face, enjoying your own athleticism as you explore a new mountain, is an extraordinary experience. And this participatory sport experience can be realistically shared with children as young as five years old (once you're off the bunny hill) and continues to be a sport one can enjoy long past retirement age. It is little wonder that sliding down a snowy mountain is such a cherished experience by millions of families throughout the globe.

I also learned from our experiences not to underestimate my children. They were capable of travelling further than many adults would want or like to travel. They were happy to put in the time to become better skiers than most adults. They were excited to learn the myriad of skills to travel in avalanche prone and crevasse filled terrain. They might only be children, but they could be tough like Heather and me. However, I also learned that they had limits. They were still children who could be moody and occasionally overwhelmed by the experience.

Similarly, my children learned about me. Like many children view their parents, my kids often saw me as a minor deity. Considering we were chasing a ski goal, my ski knowledge, my ski skills, and my ski connections continued to impress them. But they also saw my foibles and weaknesses. I struggled to drive on the wrong side of the road in Australia. I made stupid mistakes – from putting my passport through the laundry to putting regular gas into a diesel vehicle. And I struggled to be mindful enough to address my bitter disappointment as Keira and I were quarantined in Africa seemingly without a chance to complete our goal in time. For better or worse, my kids saw my weaknesses, not just my strengths.

Perhaps most importantly of all the lessons, however, was how I learned how good random people are in this world. A family we never knew helped get our car into a repair shop in Coomo, Australia. Distant connections welcomed us into their house and put us up while we were stuck in South Africa. A random waiter treated Heather as a genuine equal human being in a land where such actions were rare. A hotel concierge provided emotional support and friendship as we were distraught and quarantined. The mother of the world record holder we displaced, instead of begrudging us, warmly congratulated us with open arms.

In a world in which we are bombarded by traditional and social media of images of division, hate, and violence – our travels were a continual reminder that most people are loving, sweet, and compassionate. Is there a better lesson one could learn while travelling to the far corners of the earth with kids trying to twice break a world record?

Appendix I

Latitude, Elevation, and Skiing

There are some topics that are too ski geeky to be part of the main part of the book itself, but which as a ski geek I wanted to somehow include. So, I have created a few appendices to capture some of the ski geeky information about skiing around the world.[4]

---

[4] I also toyed with the idea of having a full appendix section on why I chose the quotes that I did to start each chapter, but ultimately decided that doing so would be too self-indulgent. So, I've relegated this self-indulgence to a paragraph, which is this footnote. It seemed only fitting that I extensively quote the legendary Japanese extreme skier Yuichiro Miura, who is not only one of the great skiers of all times, but also perhaps the greatest philosopher and poet on skiing. And frequently throughout our adventures I would think of my favorite poem – Alfred Lord Tennyson's *Ulysses*. Inspired by both Homer's Odyssey and Dante's The Divine Comedy, the poem is a speech by Ulysses (also known as Odysseus) as an older man on why he is bored with his ordinary life as a king, and why he yearns for adventure and excitement again. From wanting to drink life to the lees, to bemoaning how dull it is to pause, to wanting to chase knowledge like a shooting star, Tennyson's poem speaks to me like nothing else I have ever read. Naturally, I thought it was appropriate to begin many chapters with this great poem. For those who are familiar with the poem – it is worth noting that its references to Odysseus' wife and son have no relationship to my wife and kids. I do not see Heather like Odysseus' wife, and I do not see Keira and Maddock like Odysseus' son. Rather, to the extent that I would analogize us to characters in the poem, all four of us, and especially me, are more equivalent to Odysseus' mariners, the fellow adventurers to whom his speech is directed. Let me end this footnote with Tennyson's immortal ending

In order to ski, one needs hills or mountains, and sufficiently cold temperatures for it to snow (or to make artificial snow using snow guns). While numerous factors play into temperatures – e.g., ocean currents, distance to ocean, prevailing winds, etc. – the two biggest factors in getting colder temperatures are (i) increasing latitude, and (ii) increasing elevation. This makes intuitive sense – the further one goes away from the equator towards the poles, the colder it gets. Similarly, the higher one goes in elevation, the colder it gets. That's why mountains are snowcapped, and valleys are not.

While it's not fair to reduce a complicated and varying rate to a single number, a very rough rule of thumb is that it gets 4 degrees (Fahrenheit) colder for every thousand feet of elevation gain (this temperature change is referred to by atmospheric scientists as the lapse rate). Similarly, and please take this number with an even larger grain of salt, the temperature decreases by roughly 1.5 degrees (Fahrenheit) for every one degree of latitude gained.

As such, for the most snow-challenged continent, Africa, its ski areas lie either at high elevation near the far northern tip and the southern tip. On the opposite end, as one gets too high in elevation or too close to the poles, frigid weather impedes skiing. So, for example, we had to ski Antarctica not in its winter, but in the middle of its summer.

For those curious (which may just be me), I put together a quick table of where the kids and I skied by rough latitude (rounded to the nearest degree) and base elevation (rounded to the nearest 100'). As we've skied a wide variety of places in North America, I chose the furthest south and furthest north major ski areas.

And also, although treeline is indicative primarily of summer temperatures and a few other factors, I find treeline not only fascinating but impactful on skiing. So, I note whether the skiing is above treeline, below treeline, or a mix.

---

to the poem, particularly apt as I am no longer young: "and tho we are not now that strength which in old days moved earth and heaven, that which we are, we are; One equal temper of heroic hearts, made weak by time and fate, but strong in will, to strive, to seek, to find, and not to yield."

Continent	Location	Latitude	Base Elevation	Ski Area / Skiing Compared to Treeline
Africa	Oukaimeden	31° N	8,500'	Above
Antarctica	Wolf's Fang	71° S	3,600'	Above
Antarctica	Antarctic Peninsula	65° S	0'	Above
Asia	Yongpyong	38° N	2,500'	Below
Australia	Thredbo	36° S	4,500'	Mostly Below
Europe	Cervinia	46° N	6,600'	Mostly Above
North America (furthest north)	Alyeska	61° N	300'	Mostly Above
North America (furthest south)	Ski Santa Fe	35° N	10,400'	Mostly Below
South America (north)	Valle Nevado	33° S	9,800'	Above
South America (south)	Martial Glacier	55° S	2,000'	Above

Appendix II

Relative Height of the Mountain Ranges

When one stands in Denver and stares up at the beautiful Rocky Mountains, they are truly impressive peaks towering over the Denver skyline. But as we travelled to comparable towns such as Marrakesh and Santiago, the peaks of the Atlas Mountains and the Andes Mountains seemed even more impressive. How can one objectively compare the size of this differential?

Here is a chart of the locations we skied at, showing the vertical differential from town to summit of the highest nearby mountain. So, this chart provides the elevation of the nearby town, city, or in the case of Antarctica the ice sheet runway at the base of the mountains. Then, it provides the elevation of the highest nearby mountain. This highpoint is often a rocky summit of a peak, not the top of the ski area or backcountry skiing location that is typically much lower. And please bear in mind that the locations are somewhat subjective, both as to the choice of town / city at the base of the mountains and choice of tall nearby mountain. Nevertheless, hopefully this chart provides a comparison on the size of the mountains we saw during our adventures. All numbers are rounded to the nearest 100'.

Putting pen to paper, I was not too surprised to see that the Andes, Alps, and Atlas Mountains all proved bigger than my beloved Rocky Mountains. That said, I was surprised to see that the Andes were more than twice the height differential compared to my home mountain range of the Rockies.

It was hardly surprising that the smallest mountain range was in South Korea, with Australia being the second smallest. However, I was surprised that the elevation differential in Antarctica was less than the Rocky Mountains. The Antarctica mountains, like Wolf's Fang (a/k/a Ulvetanna Peak) were far more impressive than our mountains in Colorado. And I know this chart is unfair to Asia as we chose to ski in South Korea as opposed to Kashmir.

Anyhow, here is the chart.

Continent	Town at Base of Mountains	Elevation of Town	Highest Nearby Mountain	Elevation of Mountain	Vertical Differential
Africa	Marrakesh	1,500'	Toubkal	13,700'	12,200'
Antarctica	[Wolf's Fang Runway]	3,600'	Ulvetanna Peak	9,600'	6,000
Asia	PyeongChang	2,500'	Seoraksan	5,600'	3,100
Australia	Jindabyne	3,000'	Mount Kosciuszko	7,300'	4,300'
Europe	Ivrea	800'	Mont Blanc	15,800'	15,000'
North America	Denver	5,300'	Mount Evans	14,300'	9,000'
South America	Santiago	1,900'	Aconcagua	22,800'	20,900'

Appendix III

The Extent of Skiing on Each Continent

While there's snow on every continent on earth, the amount of skiing varies wildly. This appendix will briefly review how much skiing (at ski areas) is available on each continent (and by region), in descending order based upon three major statistics. The typical ways to measure the extent of skiing (which are also the only easy numbers to find) are by (i) the number of ski areas, (ii) the kilometers of ski trails (a European measure), and/or (iii) the number of ski lifts.

Even though most of Earth's snow and ice is on Antarctica, there are no formal ski areas in Antarctica, so this appendix lists Antarctica last, though it's by no means last in terms of skiing.

Here are the current stats, rounded to the nearest fifty (except for Africa as all numbers would round to zero), courtesy of www.skiresort.info.

- Europe: 4,000 ski areas, with 38,450 kilometers of slopes, and 16,750 lifts.
- North America: 800 ski areas, with 15,450 kilometers of slopes, and 3,750 lifts.
- Asia: 1,250 ski areas, with 5,200 kilometers of slopes, and 3,150 lifts.
- South America: 50 ski areas, with 700 kilometers of slopes, and 300 lifts.
- Australia and Oceania: 50 ski areas, with 650 kilometers of slopes, and 250 lifts.

- Africa: 7 ski areas, with 19 kilometers of slopes, and 23 lifts.
- Antarctica: 0 ski areas, with 0 kilometers of slopes, and 0 lifts (but lots of snow).

How does the United States compare to other countries? Well, using the same three factors, and adding up the percentage of worldwide skiing for each factor, here are the top five countries in the world in descending order:

- United States: 500 ski areas, with 11,450 kilometers of slopes, and 2,900 lifts.
- France: 250 ski areas, with 10,150 kilometers of slopes, and 3,150 lifts.
- Austria: 450 ski areas, with 7,250 kilometers of slopes, and 2,600 lifts.
- Switzerland: 350 ski areas, with 7,150 kilometers of slopes, and 1,850 lifts.
- Japan: 550 ski areas, with 3,100 kilometers of slopes, and 1,900 lifts.

Although the United States has the most skiing of any country, let's not forget that in spite of Switzerland's population of less than 9 million people, it has roughly three quarters of the skiing that the entire United States has. And, if the European Union was considered a country, it would be far and away first, followed by the United States, Switzerland, Japan, and Canada.

Skier visit numbers offer a similar but not identical picture to the amount of skiing offered by country, with the best estimates that the top five countries in descending order are currently the United States, Austria, France, Japan, and Italy. And if the European Union was considered a country, it would be first, followed by the United States, Japan, Switzerland, and Canada.

If we were just to look at my beloved home state of Colorado, it tops the rankings of states and provinces in the English-speaking world. Using the above metrics on extent of skiing, the top five US states / Canadian provinces, all of which have much more skiing than either Australia or New Zealand, are in descending order: Colorado, British Columbia, Quebec, California, and Utah. (And yes, I know that technically Quebec is not a part of the English-speaking world.) If Colorado was its own country, it would come in twelfth place overall in the world, with roughly two percent of the world's skiing.

Appendix IV

Best of List by Continent

"Best of" lists are inherently unreliable as they are based upon the subjective experiences of the author. Compounding this problem in this case is that my kids and I have skied extensively throughout North America, but only skimmed the surface of skiing on the other continents. Of course, we did hit some of the best resorts on each continent (other than Asia). As such, I do have some ability to compare the best to the best. However, with regards to Asia, this list could be rather different if we chose to ski at the Himalayan ski resort of Gulmarg in Kashmir as opposed to Yongpyong and Jisan in South Korea.

As one who is not shy to share his opinions, for better or worse, here is my list of the "best of" skiing comparing the continents based upon what I've seen.

Best Views:
   Winner: Antarctica
   Runner up: Europe

Best Nearby Wildlife:
   Winner: Antarctica
   Runner up: Australia

Best Snow Quality:
   Winner: North America
   Runner up: South America

Biggest Ski Resorts:
    Winner: Europe
    Runner up: North America

Biggest Mountain Ranges:
    Winner: South America
    Runner up: Europe

Best Food:
    Winner: Asia
    Runner up: Europe

Best Wine:[5]
    Winner: Europe
    Runner up: Australia

Best Customer Service:
    Winner: Asia
    Runner up: North America

Friendliest Fellow Skiers:
    Winner: Asia
    Runner up: Australia

Most exotic:
    Winner: Antarctica
    Runner up: Africa

---

[5]   As we used South Africa as a jumping off point only for Antarctica, when judging the best wine, for the continent of Africa I'm considering Moroccan wine only. If South Africa was included, Africa would likely nudge out Australia in my humble opinion as the second-best wine.

About the Author

Jordan Lipp is an attorney who lives in Golden, Colorado with his wife and two children. In addition to his day job, Jordan is also a volunteer ski patroller, avalanche safety instructor, and the author of two prior books on skiing: *Hunting Powder: A Skier's Guide to Finding Colorado's Best Snow* (2021) and *Backcountry Skiing Berthoud Pass: A Guidebook to Skiing and Snowboarding Berthoud Pass, Colorado* (2005). Beyond the world of skiing, along with his wife, he authored the book: *Is There Apple Juice in My Wine? Thirty-Eight Laws that Affect the Wine You Drink* (2018), and he also authored the legal book, *Product Liability Law & Procedure in Colorado* (2015).